SUPERPUMP!

SUPERPUMP!

Hardcore Women's Bodybuilding

Ben Weider, C.M., & Robert Kennedy

Sterling Publishing Co., Inc. New York

Edited by Robert Hernandez
Designed by Jim Anderson

Library of Congress Cataloging-in-Publication Data

Weider, Ben, 1923–
   Superpump!   :   hardcore women's bodybuilding.

   Includes index.
   1. Bodybuilding for women.   2. Women bodybuilders—
Interviews.   I. Kennedy, Robert, 1938–
II. Title.
GV546.6.W64W434   1986   646.7'5   86-6034
ISBN 0-8069-4800-0 (pbk.)

Copyright © 1986 by Ben Weider and Robert Kennedy
Published by Sterling Publishing Co., Inc.
Two Park Avenue, New York, N.Y. 10016
Distributed in Canada by Oak Tree Press Ltd.
% Canadian Manda Group, P.O. Box 920, Station U
Toronto, Ontario, Canada M8Z 5P9
Distributed in the United Kingdom by Blandford Press
Link House, West Street, Poole, Dorset BH15 1LL, England
Distributed in Australia by Capricorn Ltd.
P.O. Box 665, Lane Cove, NSW 2066
Manufactured in the United States of America
All rights reserved.

CONTENTS

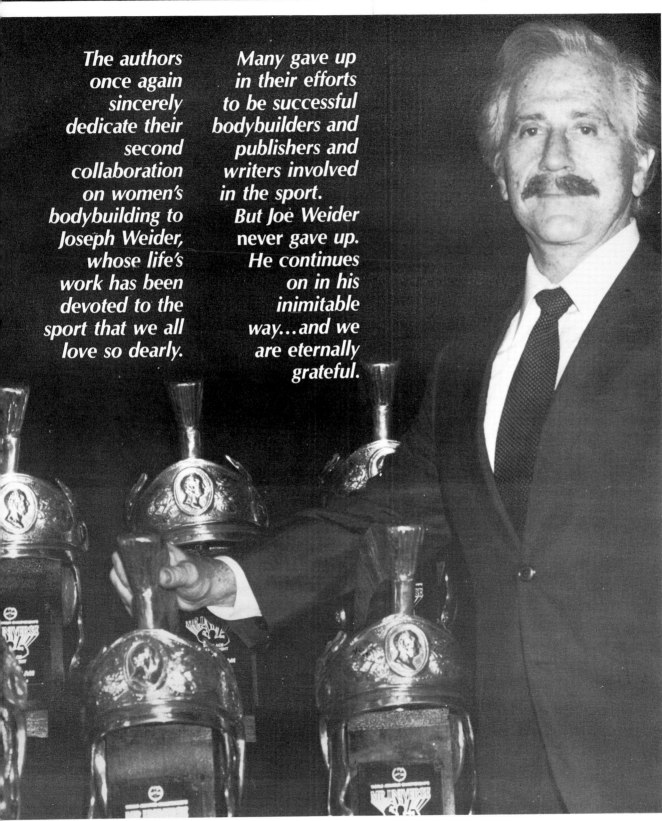

The authors once again sincerely dedicate their second collaboration on women's bodybuilding to Joseph Weider, whose life's work has been devoted to the sport that we all love so dearly.

Many gave up in their efforts to be successful bodybuilders and publishers and writers involved in the sport. But Joe Weider never gave up. He continues on in his inimitable way...and we are eternally grateful.

Acknowledgments

The production of a successful book is never the work of just one or two people. A book is the sum total of many contributions. Accordingly, we would first like to thank our editor at Sterling Publishing Co., Inc., Robert Hernandez, for his patience and untiring efforts to polish and shape the manuscript, and to Jim Anderson, who designed the book.

To Joe Weider, we offer our sincerest gratitude and appreciation, not only for making the Weider photo library available, but also for his ongoing efforts to make bodybuilding a sport of which we can all be proud. It has not been easy. For years, bodybuilding was an unrecognized activity with little hope of becoming a legitimate sport with positive press coverage. We will never forget that Joe Weider, through the pages of Muscle & Fitness *magazine, changed the course of bodybuilding. He alone made it happen.*

We would also like to acknowledge the excellent photography of Mike Neveaux, John Balik, Chris Lund, Steve Douglas, Bill Heimanson, Doris Barrilleaux, Dick Zimmerman, Harry Langdon, Peter Brenner, Luc Ekstein, Bob Gardner, Reg Bradford, Bruce Curtis and Bill Dobbins.

INTRODUCTION

The President of the International Olympic Committee, Juan Antonio Samaranch, receives from Ben Weider, C.M., President of the International Federation of Bodybuilders, the Distinguished Service Award. This honor is presented to individuals who have dedicated their lives towards the promotion of physical fitness.

People who love bodybuilding are almost body worshippers. We know because we joined the club many years ago. It is not, by any means, an exclusive one. There are millions of us, but it is an ardent group with one common goal: To keep our bodies in the best shape possible by pumping iron. Of course, youth has it over us old-timers, but you can still be as enthusiastic as the years roll by.

Women's bodybuilding is more popular today than ever. At last, it has achieved worldwide recognition. It is satisfying to know that what we have believed in for so long has now gained total acceptance. It is estimated that there are over 40 million weight trainers in the free world—19 million in North America alone.

Bodybuilding, using free weights and machines to shape and tone muscles, is the fastest way known to transform the female figure. You can use these modern bodybuilding methods to reshape your body.

Right now, whether you are tall or short, fat or thin, young or not so young, you can use progressive-resistance exercise (weight training) to advantage. Work out conscientiously and you will notice changes within three to five weeks. Keep at it and the sky's the limit. You get out of bodybuilding what you are prepared to put into it. Using the latest facts about nutrition and exercise techniques revealed in the following pages, you will have the formula for personal success. Study the routines, diets, secrets, and

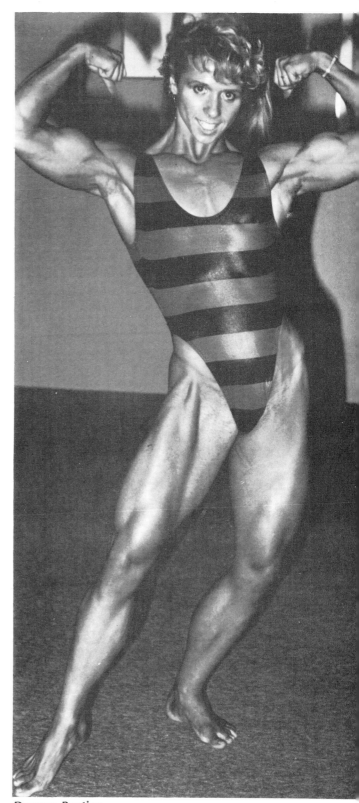

Deanna Panting

tips that the champions themselves have used to gain their own success and you will be on your way.

In order to accomplish your goals, you must know where to begin. We are not suggesting that if, for example, you are a beginner to bodybuilding, you try and follow a champion's routine. That is not the way to make your mark in this sport.

Inevitably, you should start not only with light weights but also with a short routine. Needless to say, if you are new to rigorous exercise or haven't followed a workout program for some considerable time, then you should get a checkup from your doctor. Tell her that you want to start weight training. If there is any doubt about your current state of health—and if there is a history of heart disease, high-blood pressure, cholesterol, or other organic problems—then ask for a stress test to check out your condition. Inform your doctor of any real or inherited problems. This goes for any new diet you may want to start. Your physician's approval is the safest and most sensible way to begin. Once you have this, you will be all the more happy, knowing that you can devote your attention to shaping your body with modern weight-training methods.

You would not be reading these words if you did not want to improve your physical appearance. Accept your wish for a great-looking body and with the valuable facts revealed in this book—by the top names in women's bodybuilding—you can take your own body to its highest potential. Whether you want to walk down the street and turn everyone's head in admiration, or take the sport of bodybuilding face on and compete to be an IFBB Ms. Olympia winner . . . the choice is yours.

Wherever you go in the world, you will see a variety of magazines dealing with the subject of women's bodybuilding—*Muscle & Fitness*, *Flex*, *Shape*, *MuscleMag International*, and *Sports Fitness*. Read all you can on the subject, but avoid those periodicals that do not seem to be totally immersed in the sport. A previous book by us entitled *Pumping Up! Super Shaping the Feminine Physique* (Sterling Publishing Co., Inc., 2 Park Avenue, New York, NY, 10016) has proven to be not only a runaway bestseller on the subject of women's bodybuilding, but an authoritative work deemed among the best yet turned into print. Certainly *Pumping Up!* is required reading for all women who want to pursue physical excellence through the bodybuilding way of life. We are determined to bring you the best information possible, updated advice that can inspire you to your own personal success.

The women interviewed in this book were chosen specifically for their individual views of the relatively new sport of bodybuilding for women. We asked about their training and how they first got involved in it. We questioned their feelings about the sport and the direction it is taking. The frankness of their opinions is evident.

As you read on, you will notice how each woman has overcome personal difficulties and adversities. There is a strong feeling of individualism among our subjects. And there is also a staunch resolve to *never* give up. Each woman has maintained her true love for training. In many cases, it comes down to a desire for physical expression and regular workouts. All of the champions are devoted to the sport of pumping iron . . . and thrill at their own obligation to keep physically perfect and powerfully strong. Each workout is like a delightful tonic that gives measurable physical results and immeasurable self-fulfillment. Welcome to the club.

Thanks to the efforts of IFBB President Ben Weider, bodybuilding is now popular in China. The Asian Olympic Committee has recognized bodybuilding officially.

THE ADDED FACTORS

Jose Baumgartner

Superpump! is unique because it relays the thoughts and practices of the world's top women bodybuilders in addition to the views of the authors. *Superpump!* goes one step further, offering advice and techniques for the more experienced weight trainers. It's the logical step after reading *Pumping Up!*, but it can also stand on its own merit.

Nothing we write is the last word in bodybuilding know-how. What we offer, however, is experience. We have attended thousands of bodybuilding shows, known hundreds of personalities, observed training practices worldwide, as well as conducted research seminars on the diet and exercise programs of the most successful bodybuilders. We both train regularly and with as much enthusiasm as ever. It continues to be not only our life's work but also our most absorbing hobby.

Let's briefly review a few important aspects of the sport of bodybuilding.

Warming Up

Never neglect to warm up your muscles before training. There are two initial warm-ups. The first is to prepare your heart and lungs for strenuous effort. You can do this by riding a stationary bike or by jumping rope. In a short time (2–10 minutes) your blood will be circulating faster through your veins. It makes you really *want* to train.

Next do some basic stretches (3–6 minutes). Everybody has favorites. Let in-

stinct prevail. Stretch from side to side, from top to bottom. Do not bounce or stretch beyond your limits. Easy does it. First reach for one leg, then the other. Stretch upwards. Stretch downwards. Test the extremities of a variety of positions, always with that element of unhurried moderation. You should *feel* the stress for a count of 8–12 seconds and repeat each stretch several times. Test the flexibility of your back, shoulders, arms, and legs.

The most vital form of warm-up is to precede each bodybuilding exercise with a set of repetitions using only a moderate weight. This will prepare your muscles for the heavier, more demanding sets to follow. For example, if your best bench press is eight reps with 120 pounds, then a preliminary warm-up set with 60–80 pounds is a good way to start. Only one warm-up set is necessary; most warm-up sets involve slightly higher repetitions—say 12–15.

Exercise Style

The key word is *strict*. For the most part, good exercise form is important. For example, Juliette Bergman, an up-and-coming female bodybuilder, takes about two seconds to perform the positive part of an exercise (lifting the weight) and four or five seconds to finish the negative aspect (lowering it to the starting position).

Remember that fast (pumping) movements tend to rely on momentum to get the weight up, rather than muscle power. The golden rule about exercise performance is simply that you should use the style that will best fully stimulate your muscles. This means for the most part that your exercises should be performed strictly, using a full range of motion, lifting and lowering the weight in a controlled and smooth fashion. Occasionally, there is merit in using less strict form in some movements. This is called *creative cheating*.

Sleep and Relaxation

Bodybuilding is a very strenuous activity. It can take little more than half a minute of your time to lift a hundred-pound barbell for ten repetitions, yet at its conclusion you will have lifted an incredible *one thousand pounds*! No other pastime makes more demands on your muscles. Accordingly, rest and sleep are an important part of your program. You need to relax to give your muscles time to recuperate and grow. Try to get seven or eight hours' sleep each night, and, if possible, put your feet up and relax at times during the day, especially after meals. Those women who want to gain weight will find it difficult if they play tennis before a workout, or go dancing afterwards. Muscles need rest to recover. Stress results in overworked adrenal glands, at which time bodybuilding progress will come to a halt.

Concentration and Consistency

Concentrate from the moment you begin your workout. Do not engage in conversation between sets of exercise. If you must talk, then do so after you have completed training a particular body part.

Gladys Portugues does an incline bench press.

Listen to champion bodybuilder Robby Robinson: "A perfect rep requires the use of a great deal of mental concentration. You have to think intensity into every repetition. Contract the muscle you are exercising as hard as you can during each rep. This is a painful way to train but it yields results."

Finally, use your concentration to mentally direct the work load into a specific area. For example, if you are chinning yourself to build your biceps, then concentrate on willing your biceps to *feel* the action. Alternatively, if you are chinning to improve your lat muscles, then *think* the action into your back area.

Probably the single most important aspect of successful bodybuilding is consistency. Do not miss workouts. Naturally, if you are sick or genuinely over-tired, you should not train. On the other hand, to miss a workout through laziness is not the way to a well-toned body. In addition to consistent workouts, you should also apply consistency of effort. Once you have mastered the art of consistent high-intensity training, you hold in your hands the secret to reaching the top.

Goal Setting

Set small goals for yourself as you progress in bodybuilding. To aspire to being a six-time Ms. Olympia before you have even won a local contest is unrealistic. Set yourself attainable goals, and work to reach them one at a time. As soon as you reach a goal, you can set another higher one.

It is far easier for your mind (and your muscles) to achieve small step-by-step goals than to aspire to the moon in one gigantic step towards the heavens. A thousand-mile journey begins with the

Laura Beaudry

Mary Roberts

first step. Go for the top by all means, but do it via a workable series of realistically achievable goals.

Self-Analysis

Be observant. Learn about yourself. Champion bodybuilders, like famous models or top actresses, are usually very aware of how they look to others. You should make a habit of becoming self-critical; learn the art of objectively analyzing your physique. The use of a mirror is helpful, but you may see only what you want to see. A scale can be even more deceiving—it doesn't tell you how you look. The best way to judge yourself is to have photographs taken at regular intervals from all angles. Study them at home; do not ask your friends for their opinions. Decide for yourself what you want your body to look like.

When you have a glaring weakness, work on it harder, and bring it up to par with the rest of your body. Train the weak area first in your workout (the Weider priority system) with more exercises, more sets, and more intensity until you are satisfied.

Overtraining

As you continue to train, you will discover new exercises. Often you will incorporate them into your workout. You hate the idea of dropping an exercise, so your workouts get longer and longer. You add more sets and spend more time in the gym. After a few weeks, progress comes to a standstill. You become disillusioned. The excitement vanishes from your workouts. You have overtrained. A muscle that is continually worked before it fully recuperates will become stringy and will probably lose size and strength. Control your urge to add more and more exercises to your routine. It is far better to substitute exercises than to create a mammoth-sized routine that will bore you and result in overtrained muscles.

Confidence

It's a good idea to develop a healthy amount of genuine confidence. You are in a tough sport and this ingredient is vital. Who can deny that champions like Rachel McLish and Corinna Everson are confident? It adds to their charm and charisma. What turns people off, of course, is an overconfident, conceited attitude, which you should avoid, or else your friends will avoid you.

Nurture confidence by telling yourself that you will be the best you can be. Do more thah try to be the best. The notion of trying admits the possibility of failure. Tell yourself that you *will* go all the way. Believe in yourself with a strong, quiet confidence.

Drug Abuse

Abusing your body by smoking cigarettes, drinking alcohol, or taking drugs will hold you back from being the ultimate champion. If you currently indulge in any of these bad habits, then make every effort to get them out of your life or under control. An occasional glass of wine is acceptable; tobacco and drugs are not. Your most valuable possession is your vitality. It is the most wonderful gift of nature. To possess robust health is not just for the young. With good natural food, vigorous, regular exercise, and a lifestyle free of self-destructive habits, good health can stay with you for your whole life.

Rachel McLish performs a triceps extension with a dumbbell.

There are numerous exercise principles that can be used to increase the effectiveness of your workouts. Some may seem to conflict with one another; others may not appear to be practical. However, all of the following have been used successfully by the world's greatest bodybuilders at one time or another.

Supersets

A superset is the alternation of two exercises, one after the other, without rest. These two exercises should involve opposing muscle groups. A typical superset for your arm muscles would be the alternation of a biceps exercise with a triceps movement.

Supersets are more difficult to do than straight sets (the performance of several sets of the same exercise). They can save time in the gym and help in obtaining a faster muscle pump in a given area.

Trisets

This principle involves the performance of three exercises for one body part, all in quick succession. It is an advanced technique that greatly adds to the intensity of your workout. Trisets are seldom used for long periods, but are usually employed for 3–5 weeks to shock a muscle group into new growth.

The following is an example of a triset for the biceps area. No rest is taken between the following three exercises:

1. Barbell Curl
2. Incline Dumbbell Curl
3. Seated Alternate Dumbbell Curl

You will find that two or three trisets will really cause a selected muscle area to "burn" . . . and grow.

Giant Sets

This Weider principle takes trisets a step further. Giant sets involve the performance of 4–6 movements with no rest between them. They are extremely intense and should only be done at selected periods throughout your training year. The following is an example of giant sets for the triceps muscle:

1. Standing Triceps Stretch
2. Triceps Kickback
3. Lying Triceps Curl
4. Parallel Bar Dip
5. Triceps Pulley Pushdown

There is a degree of differing opinions among the stars of bodybuilding as to the merits of giant sets. Some champions feel that they are useful to break the growth barrier, to reach a new plateau, whereas others feel that the resulting intensity is too severe and can cause muscle breakdown.

Negative Reps

This is a very popular method with hardcore women bodybuilders. Many use negative reps, at least *some* of the time. The negative aspect of the repetition is the downwards movement, or lowering the weight that you lift. According to German physiological scientific experiments, the negative aspect of a lift, if resisted with an intense energy, can contribute greatly to strength and size increases.

To perform a negative rep, you will need a training partner (or two) to lift a weight 25–45 percent heavier than you normally use. After the weight has been

Penny Price

Anita Gandol

"lifted" into position, begin to lower it slowly on your own, strongly resisting the downward momentum. Of course, you do not need training partners to benefit from the negative part of an exercise. If you are training alone, we suggest you merely endeavor to slow down the downward part of a repetition to the extent that you are struggling to hold the weight under control as you do so.

Continuous Tension

This principle was introduced many years ago in Joe Weider's *Muscle Builder/ Power* magazine. It has remained popular ever since. As the name suggests, it involves using any exercise where the tension or stress on a particular muscle is kept at a high level. You do not rest during a continuous-tension repetition. To apply this technique, squats, triceps extensions, bench presses, standing presses, parallel bar dips, etc., would all be performed *without* completely straightening the limbs in question. In this way the muscles are never free of forceful contraction during the entire set of an exercise.

Isotension

Don't confuse isotension (the word was invented by Joe Weider) with low-intensity muscle flexing or muscle control. Isotension is the complete flexing (even to the point of cramping) then loosening and relaxing of the muscle. To perform isotension movements, flex a chosen muscle as hard as you can during the last three or four repetitions of an exercise. Forget about lifting the weight. Concentrate on stressing the muscles excessively during the last part of the set.

Triple Dropping

Sometimes this method is known as the *stripping method*. Like several other principles, it takes you beyond the point of normal fatigue or failure in your exercises. Let's take the bench press as an example of how the triple-dropping method works:

Assume you are training with 100 pounds and have managed a maximum of five repetitions with this weight. Immediately have two training partners strip off a ten-pound disc from either side. This will enable you to perform several more repetitions until once more you are at the point of muscle failure. Again have your helpers remove (in unison) two more ten-pound discs. Now continue to train for several more repetitions, and so on. You will end up with an almighty burning sensation, and additional muscle growth will surely come your way.

Another method of reducing your poundage in this way would be to train with dumbbells "down the rack." For example, start curling with a pair of twenty-pound dumbbells. When you reach muscle failure, pop them back on the rack and grab a pair of fifteen-pound dumbbells. Continue for several more reps. When you can't do any more, exchange the dumbbells for a pair of ten-pounders. Continue once again, until muscle failure.

Specialization Routines

If you have a particular body part that is lacking in development, you need to adopt a specialization routine. For example, if your thighs are underdeveloped, you may want to devote more of your workout time to training them with additional exercises and sets. To compensate for the additional time, you would cut down on the number of sets you performed for your better-developed body parts. A thigh-specialization routine would be to perform five sets of squats, hack lifts, leg curls, leg presses, lunges, and sissy squats, whereas you would usually do only half this number of thigh movements.

Gladys Portugues

STARTING YOUR WORKOUT

Carla Dunlap

Beginners should use *only* the bar for their first workout—without putting any weights on it. As time goes by, you can add small discs on a regular basis, but never so much weight that the exercises cannot be performed smoothly. For more information about beginner's routines, exercise explanations, techniques, recommended equipment, nutrition, frequency, and other tips, read our previous book, *Pumping Up! Super Shaping the Feminine Physique* (Sterling Publishing Co., Inc., New York).

As a beginning bodybuilder, it is suggested that you train three times a week. Mondays, Wednesdays, and Fridays are ideal because your weekends will be free. Train your whole body on each of the three days. Perform one exercise for each body part. Rest two or three minutes between each set of exercise. Start with just a single set of each movement the first two weeks. Then progress to two sets of each exercise for two more weeks, and finally do three sets of each exercise. Perform your exercises in good, strict style. Never bounce or heave the weight.

Clare Furr does leg raises for a tight midsection.

The Beginner's Routine

Candy Csencsits

Warm-Up
(Heart Pulse)

Rope Jumping
(1½ minutes)
This is a good way to begin your routine because it increases your blood circulation and warms up your muscles for exercise.

Deltoids
(Shoulders)

Dumbbell Press
(3 sets × 8 reps)
While in the standing position as shown, hold two dumbbells at the shoulders. Keep your back straight and your head up. Press both dumbbells simultaneously to the overhead position. Do not lean backwards during the exercise. Lower and repeat with a steady rhythm.

Pectorals
(Chest)

Bench Press
(3 sets × 8 reps)
The standard way of performing the bench press is to lie face up on a bench. Take a grip, with your thumbs under the bar and about 2 feet (60 cm) apart, which allows the forearms to be vertical when the upper arms are parallel to the floor.

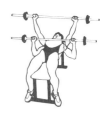

Lower the weight from the straight-arm position to the pectorals. Touch the bar lightly on the chest (no bouncing) and press upwards. Keep your elbows under the bar, and don't allow them to come close to the body.

Beginners may find that the bar starts to fall either forward or backwards, or that the weight rises unevenly because one arm is stronger than the other. Time and practice will cure these minor faults.

When you lower the bar to your chest, don't allow it to drop! Always control its descent deliberately, especially if it is a heavy weight.

Thighs

Squat
(3 sets × 10 reps)

Take a barbell from a pair of squat racks and hold it at the back of your neck. You may roll a towel around the bar for added comfort. If needed, place your heels on a two-by-four-inch block of wood to improve balance. Some people just cannot squat flat-footed. It forces them to adopt a very wide stance and, even so, they are forced to lean too far forward when squatting down. Breathe in deeply before squatting. Keep your back flat and your head up throughout the movement. Breathe out forcefully as you raise upwards.

Lats
(Upper Back)

Wide-grip Pulldown
(3 sets × 10 reps)

This exercise has to be performed on a lat machine. Take a wide over-grip on the bar, and pull down as far as you can. This exercise is not as effective as the wide-grip chinning exercise, but it does have the advantage that you can use less resistance and pull the bar lower, working your lats over a greater range of movement. You may pull to the front or the back of the neck.

Kay Baxter performs some heavy-duty squats.

Abdominals
(Midsection)

Bench Crunch
(3 sets × 15 reps)

Lie on your back on the floor. Your calves should rest on a bench in such a way that your thighs are vertical. Place your hands behind your head and slowly attempt to sit up. Because of the fixed position of the legs, the maximum contraction is not passed over as in the regular sit-up movement (not recommended). There is constant tension in the middle and upper abdominals.

Triceps
(Back of Arms)

Lying Triceps Stretch
(3 sets × 10 reps)

Lie on your back on a flat bench as shown, and hold two dumbbells at arm's length above your chest. Keeping the upper arm as vertical as possible, lower the dumbbells slowly to your ears, and raise again to the starting position. This exercise works the entire triceps area. Do not use heavy weights in this exercise if you are prone to elbow soreness.

Lynn Conkwright works out her own kind of tummy training.

Calves
(Lower Legs)

Standing Calf Raise
(**3 sets × 20 reps**)

It is important that the calf machine you use is capable of handling heavy weights. The apparatus should either carry a huge stack of weights or else be set up with a leverage benefit, so that comparatively small weights can add up to a large overall load.

Rise upwards and downwards on your toes with your legs straight and without bouncing at the bottom of the movement. Go for maximum stretch both in the up and down parts of the movement.

Biceps
(Front of Arms)

Barbell Curl
(**3 sets × 8 reps**)

The regular barbell curl has contributed to more big arms than any other exercise. Hold the bar slightly wider than shoulder width, and keep your elbows close to your body as you curl the weight upwards until it is under your chin.

There are two distinct styles of doing this exercise: (1) *strictly* (no leaning backwards during the movement, starting from a straight-arm position with absolutely no body motion or "swing"), and (2) *cheating* (hoisting the weight up by turning the trunk of your body into a pendulum as you swing the barbell). Both methods are workable, and most successful bodybuilders get best results

Juliette Bergman

by doing at least the first 6–8 reps in strict style and then finishing off the harder last 3–4 reps with a cheating motion.

For those of you who are past the beginner's level, we urge you to study the thoughts of each of our superstar bodybuilders. Much of what they say and do can be utilized in your training. Be cautioned, however: If you are a short, thick-set type, don't choose people like Dr. Lynne Pirie or Carolyn Cheshire as your role models. Their particular method of training may be totally unsuited to your physical type. If you have a thin, wiry body, you would be ill advised to emulate the large-muscled Deanna Panting or Kay Baxter. In bodybuilding, you are limited by your genetic boundaries. That is not to say you can't change your shape. You can. But you cannot change your basic body type.

BODYBUILDING NUTRITION

Mary Roberts and Bob Birdsong

The food you eat is immensely important to the shape of your body. If you make a habit of eating the wrong foods, sooner or later you will cause yourself health problems. Eating incorrectly can give you a range of disorders from depression and high-blood pressure to heart disease and cancer.

For each of the women bodybuilders in this book, we have listed at least one of their sample diets. These diets vary greatly. Most fall into the category of healthy nutrition. Others seem to be based on what could only be termed "junk food." In your case, if you want to be healthy and live a long and vigorous life, we suggest that you eat as best as you know how. You do not have to be a fanatic. There are occasions when all of us have to eat junk foods to be sociable and often for convenience. Many times no other food may be available, particularly when eating away from home. The best advice is to develop a taste for fresh, unprocessed foods.

The authors of this book are not health-food fanatics, but we do try to eat the most nutritious and natural foods possible. For your success in bodybuilding and for your lifetime health, we would like you to do the same.

Back in the 1970s, our message was just beginning to sift through to the general public. (Joe Weider had promoted it repeatedly through the pages of his publications.) It concerned both the role of diet in disease prevention and in the maximization of bodybuilding. Research at the time showed that animals that

Lynne Pirie

were fed high-fat, high-cholesterol diets developed blockage of their arteries. Evidence also indicated that fat and cholesterol in the food we eat influenced our cholesterol levels. Excess cholesterol clings to the artery walls and can eventually choke off blood supply to the heart. Heart attack or death can result.

Coronary heart disease is often related to a high-fat diet. Other diseases relating to the foods we eat, especially when eating is excessive, include high-blood pressure, which is the result of too much sodium and too many calories, and cerebrovascular disease (stroke) from too much cholesterol (fat).

Mary Roberts shows good form in the close-grip pulldown exercise.

Current research indicates that the healthiest eating plan is based on six food groups: whole grains, fruits, fats, vegetables, low-fat proteins, and beans, seeds, and nuts. Eat a variety of foods from each group every day. It is advised that most foods come from the four plant groups; fats and low-fat proteins should be eaten in small amounts.

Whole Grains and Potatoes

Choose from whole-grain breads, crackers, and cereals, whole wheat and vegetable pasta, oatmeal, brown rice, corn bread, tortillas, or potatoes. Eat two or three servings of this food group each day. More than half of your daily food intake can be from the carbohydrate group.

Fruits

Eat three or four pieces of fresh fruit daily. There are many to choose from: oranges, apples, grapefruit, strawberries, blueberries, bananas, peaches, pineapple, pears, grapes, plums, watermelon, cantaloupe, and many more, all of which are nutritionally beneficial and full of natural vitamins.

Fats

Limit your consumption of saturated fats to no more than 10 percent of your overall diet. Polyunsaturated vegetable oils and margarines come under this category, but do not eat more than 4–6 teaspoons per day.

Vegetables

An abundance of nutrients and fibre can be found in tomatoes, lettuce, corn, green peppers, kale, broccoli, spinach, green beans, asparagus, zucchini, brussels sprouts, turnips, squash, mushrooms, onions, carrots, cabbage, beets, peas, and beans. Eat 2–3 cups of these vegetables per day. Wash them well but do not remove the peel if at all feasible. Vegetables and fruit should always be eaten in their freshest condition.

Low-fat Proteins

Include two or three servings of low-fat dairy products in your diet each day, such as low-fat yogurt, skim milk, and cottage cheese. Eat a serving of fish, poultry, lean red meat, or low-fat hard cheese only once per day. Portions should never be large. If you eat eggs, only have one yolk for every two egg whites. Protein can constitute 15 percent of your daily diet.

Beans, Nuts, and Seeds

Try to eat 3–4 cups of beans each week, which can be kidney beans in chili, navy beans, pinto beans, baked beans, or beans in soups or salads.

Nuts and seeds can be mixed with cereals, vegetables, and fruits. However, they are high in fat (and calories), so amounts should be regulated.

Clare Furr

Junk foods . . . such as ice cream, candy, soda, desserts, pretzels, pastries, commercial cereals, chocolate, canned fruits . . . are all calorie-dense, sugar-loaded products. Alcoholic beverages of all kinds also fall into this category. High-fat/high-salt snacks, such as crackers, chips, burgers, french fries, and hot dogs, are bad news, too. File these under "occasional," which means once or twice a week only.

As a basic guideline for healthy nutrition, eat foods that are fresh and natural, without chemical additives. It's also a good idea to invest in a guide that tells you the calories in specific foods. Study the diets of the female bodybuilders that are interviewed in this book and experiment with your own eating habits. For other basic meal plans, look at the nutrition chapter in our previous book, *Pumping Up!*

DINAH ANDERSON

The Texas Rose

"I was always muscular, always had abs and biceps. I was teased so much about my muscles that I wore long sleeves wherever I went," Dinah Anderson confessed.

Circumstances have certainly changed for Dinah Anderson. Today she actively tries to improve those same muscles that brought her so much unwanted attention earlier in her life.

She was born August 29, 1952, in Janesville, Wisconsin, to a family with a brother, Bill, and a sister, Debbie. After graduating from Beloit High School in Janesville, Dinah spent a year working in England in 1972. She had the opportunity of travelling in Europe, which was a great experience for her.

Dinah didn't even start bodybuilding until 1980, but physical fitness was an important part of her life for many years before that. She was on the school gymnastics and track teams; she played volleyball and basketball. However, Dinah soon noticed that in spite of keeping up with her jogging, racquetball, and aerobics, her muscle tone was not good.

By chance, she read an article about the bodybuilder Rachel McLish and decided to join a gym and start working out. It was a Nautilus gym, and she made great progress in spite of the fact that the machines were not ideal for her height—5 feet 1½ inches.

"The first thing I said was that I didn't want to build up muscles. I just wanted improved tone. After a few weeks I was caught up in bodybuilding.

Dinah Anderson

Dinah Anderson

And I wanted more. I made such good progress that after three months I had won my first contest . . . and I went on winning. In fact, I won ten contests in a row," Ms. Anderson said to set the record straight.

At the national competition in 1981, her winning streak ended. Dinah changed gyms after the disappointment. She currently works out with free weights at Hank's Gym in Houston. Hank Bracker, the owner, helped her a lot.

"Working out with free weights instead of Nautilus was a great shock to my system. I really noticed the difference. I'm not knocking Nautilus. It is good, but in my case, I was having to use so many cushions to sit on that the exercise never felt perfect. Free weights, on the other hand, feel right. And I'm getting good results," Dinah said.

When Dinah entered her first show, she really had no idea of what to do. She copied men's posing from the magazines and just faked it. She didn't even know that she had to have a tan. She went in as white as a ghost!

Dinah usually competes at a body weight of 114 pounds. She doesn't bulk up between shows and seldom gains more than eight pounds. Right now, she hopes to compete at a slightly heavier body weight.

"I nearly always weigh between 113 and 115 pounds at a show. I'm content to make progress slowly. I never take steroids. Any improvement I make is won honestly through hard training," Dinah expressed with conviction.

The contest that Dinah is most proud of is her fifth-place finish at the Toronto World Championships in 1985. At the 1984 Ms. Olympia contest in Montreal, she had not done well, but she came back with a vengeance in Toronto.

Leg lunges . . . Dinah Anderson style.

Dinah Anderson

As well as being one of the top female bodybuilders, Dinah is also a computer programmer for a law firm. They allow her to work from 6 A.M. to 1:30 P.M. so she has plenty of time to train after work. "I usually get to the gym about 3 P.M. The best way I have found is to train chest, shoulders, and triceps one day, and legs, back, and biceps the next. My reps are usually 8–10 on the upper-body movements and 15–20 on legs. I do not do any forced reps. It's too easy to hurt yourself, especially if you train with a bad spotter. I prefer to force out my own reps. If I'm physically capable of another rep, you can bet that I'll do it. Some of my exercises are supersets. I often alternate thigh extensions with sissy squats. I need those leg cuts, and I find this combination really works," said Dinah.

Ms. Anderson really does have an unusual philosophy when it comes to diet. Unlike most women bodybuilders, she indulges in junk-food sprees. More than that, she thinks her liberal views towards eating whatever takes her fancy *helps* her progress.

"I believe that a heavy bodybuilding diet burns out some people. Personally, I love pizza, hamburgers, chocolate, candy, cookies, you name it. But, of course, I tighten up on my diet as a contest approaches. I start about eight weeks out, drop the candy and cookies, and then slowly lessen the calories. And I still always allow myself anything I want on Saturday nights.

"But even this changes during the last two weeks. Also I don't do aerobics during my off-season training. If I did, my body would get used to it, and I wouldn't get the benefit. But during the last two months I do lots of aerobics to shock my system. I run a 6½–7-minute mile and do interval sprints as well. I might do 10 sets of sprints resting only 30 seconds between each. This type of training really defines my physique more quickly than any other method I know."

Dinah intends to keep improving each year for as long as she can. Winning the Ms. Olympia contest would be fantastic, but she's a realist. Most Ms. Olympia winners are fairly tall and big, today more than ever. But don't think she'll quit trying. She's a fighter and will always do her best.

Dinah doesn't want to see the masculinization trend of women's bodybuilding continue. She hates to see women in the sport looking more like males than females.

"I love bodybuilding. And I want it to be around as a sport for a long time. True, it's a little more eccentric than some activities, but it *is* a sport, and it is tough. You train all year long to be better than you were the year before. You have to be better, or you don't place.

"But I'll stay in shape for the rest of my life, even if I give up competing . . . I'll train. I get a kick when a stranger comes up to me and tells me I look great! It makes it all worth it."

—Dinah Anderson's Diet—

Dinah Anderson prefers heavy squats for her legs.

Off-Season

6:00 A.M.

Egg sandwich
Tea

12:00 Noon

2 slices of pizza
Salad
Iced tea

3:00 P.M.

Apple

7:30 P.M.

Hamburger
French fries
3 cookies
Iced tea

—Dinah Anderson's Routine—

Frequency
Three days of consecutive training, one day of rest.

Split System
The routine is split into two parts. Chest, shoulders, and triceps are trained on day one; then she works her legs, back, and biceps on the alternate day.

Monday & Thursday

LEGS	Sets	Reps
Squat	1 ×	20
	1 ×	12–15
	1 ×	10–12
Leg Press	3 ×	8–10
Sissy Squat	3 ×	8–10
Thigh Curl	4 ×	8–10
Stiff-legged Deadlift	3 ×	8–10

BACK	Sets	Reps
Wide-grip Pulldown (Nautilus machine)	3 ×	8–10
Bent-over Rows	3 ×	8–10
Corbin Gentry Row	3 ×	8–10
High Cable Pull	3 ×	8–10

BICEPS	Sets	Reps
Dumbbell Curl	3 ×	8–10
Wide-grip Curl	3 ×	8–10
Concentration Curl	3 ×	8–10

ABDOMINALS	Sets	Reps
Crunch (weighted)	4 ×	20
Incline Crunch (weighted)	4 ×	20
Roman Chair Sit-up	3 ×	15
Nautilus Abdominal Machine	3 ×	15

Tuesday & Friday

CHEST	Sets	Reps
Bench Press	3 ×	8–10
Incline Bench Press	3 ×	8–10
Pec-Deck Flye	3 ×	8–10
Flye or	3 ×	8–10
Incline Dumbbell Press		

SHOULDERS	Sets	Reps	Pounds
Side Lateral	1 ×	3 ×	5
Raise		× 3 ×	10
(dumbbell)		× 3 ×	15*
Seated Barbell Press		3 ×	8–10
Cable Pullover		3 ×	8–10
Upright Row		3 ×	8–10
Shrug (dumbbell)		3 ×	8–10

TRICEPS	Sets	Reps
Dips (weighted)	3 ×	8–10
Lying Triceps Extension	3 ×	8–10
Cable Pressdown	3 ×	8–10
Dumbbell Kickback	3 ×	8–10

*Rest for five seconds. Then do as many reps as possible with 15-, 10-, and 5-pound dumbbells. Repeat for three sets.

Parallel bar dips work Dinah's chest and triceps muscles.

KAY BAXTER

The Female Warrior

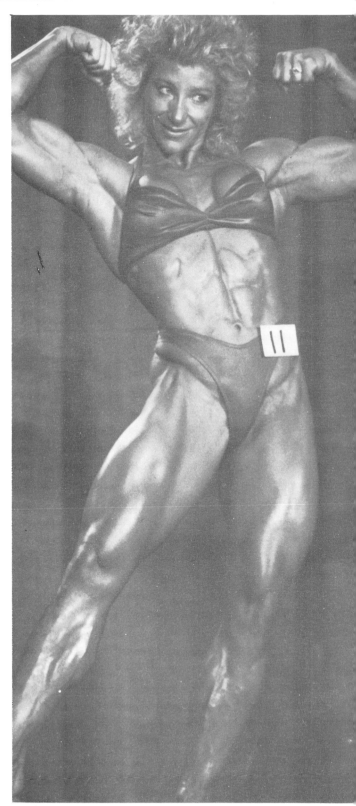

"**R**ight now I'm happier than I've ever been. I'm hitting the weights hard, studying martial arts, and learning the technique of samurai sword-handling. Deep in my heart I train for myself, not to win contests or even to please others. I train for my own satisfaction . . . and to be the ultimate female warrior," said Kay Baxter.

Kay Baxter is a different type of woman. She was born to a farming family on October 3, 1945, in Woodsfield, Ohio. She has one brother, Kenneth, and two sisters, Mavis and Joy, all of whom are considerably older than she, making her seem like an only child.

As Kay went to school in the late fifties and sixties, the world was undergoing a change, becoming more socially aware. Kay attended Kent State University. There were sit-ins and riots almost weekly. It was the students' way of life to challenge law and order and the very foundations of society. But she couldn't have cared less. She was into gymnastics, not politics.

But there is an odd twist of fate concerning this. Years later, in order to fulfill a fantasy of what it would be like to be a soldier, Kay Baxter actually joined the National Guard. And as a member of that corps, she had to study films of student uprisings, among which was film from her own college, Kent State University.

At Kent State, Kay had met her husband-to-be, got married, and moved to Toronto. She taught school and kept up with her passion for gymnastics, yoga, and aerobics (then called "slimnastics").

Look at Kay's great arm muscles!

Soon she became tired of "just fighting to be in shape to fit into last year's jeans." She wanted more. It was then that Kay went over to Toronto's biggest hardcore bodybuilding gymnasium—the Imperial—owned by competitive bodybuilder Mike DeGenova. Although the gym did not cater to women at the time, she pleaded with him to outline a routine for them.

Mike was reluctant at first, but was moved by her obvious ambition. Kay trained hard and regularly, three times a week. Her first workout, however, was a catastrophe. In her eagerness she performed three sets of each exercise instead of just one, as DeGenova had recommended. On top of that, she used very heavy weights. Returning home after the workout, Kay could hardly turn the steering wheel of her car. By the time she had got to her house, she could barely get out of the car. The next day she was so sore that moving, even slightly, was a monumental chore.

In 1978, *Muscle & Fitness* started publishing pictures of Lisa Lyon. Then there was talk of George Snyder's "Best in the World" contest. Confident that she was more muscular than the highly touted Lisa Lyon, Kay entered.

She met all the women . . . Lynne Pirie, Georgia Miller-Fudge, Laura Coombes, but still only managed tenth place. Following that, she won several amateur titles and invariably was the most applauded woman on stage. "I had always admired Laura Coombes. She had such magnificent lats. The happiest day of my life was when I found myself standing next to Laura at the 1982 Ms. Olympia. I knew I was bigger than Laura . . . and wider!" Kay said with satisfaction.

One might get the impression that Kay Baxter has a very competitive nature. Yet her goals are set and followed only to improve herself. She enters contests mainly as something to strive for and as a yardstick for her progress.

"I compete with myself. There is always something that could improve. My posing presentation, for example . . . and my legs. I have a long-time knee injury that has held back my leg training. Even today I am trying to get more cuts in my thighs. I bicycle everywhere. I run in water. I train my legs hard, but it's always a case of training around an injury," admitted Ms. Baxter.

A few years ago, Kay used to eat heartily between shows to increase her competitive body weight from 125 pounds to over 140. She doesn't do that any more. Currently, she is coaching David Lee Roth and as a year-round professional she is expected to be in shape, too. Besides, there are many jobs around right now, and she wants to be ready for them.

Kay wants to become as good as she can with her martial arts, and plans to continue her sword-handling lessons. She is already a competent horsewoman. She likes the idea of doing rock videos and has already had several offers.

Even today Kay is anxious to learn more about training. It fascinates her. She claims that bodybuilder Dr. John Gourgott is her mentor. He taught her the old-style exercises . . . like the Olympic lifters did. Kay admires the look of his physique more than anyone else's. He's from the pre-steroid era. From him she learned the proper way to chin and dip with weights . . . how to do high pulls . . . and use dumbbells correctly.

Today Kay trains in Gold's Gym in Venice, California. She said, "I love the atmosphere, the music. It's all so upbeat. I train early in the morning with two of the greatest guys—Don Ross and Kent Kuehn. They are really helpful, spot me for forced reps, negatives on dumbbell work, and keep my spirits up. I come out of a training session with them in a good mood. My routine involves training two days and taking one day of rest, then training two days followed by two days of rest. At contest time I will train five days on, two days off, then six days on, one day off as the contest approaches.

"I love bodybuilding. It's my life, but my part in it is not to conform to the current standards. In truth, I actively seek to go beyond what is asked for at a contest. Look at Arnold. He figured out what to do to win. With me, it seems that I go my own way even when I know it will not bring me the judges' votes. It's the way I am."

Ironically, since Kay is one of the most muscular and massive of all women bodybuilders, you might expect her to admire the biggest and most muscular men in the sport. That's not the case at all. She's not impressed with overly huge muscles and dead-set against the practice of taking steroids to increase size. She prefers the physiques of Samir Bannout, Bob Paris, and Brad Harris, men who have a more athletic, balanced look.

Mealtime comes at least five times a day for Kay Baxter. Her favorite foods are steak (rare), salmon (steamed), pita bread, kiwi fruit, watermelon, peaches, and lots of salads with raw vegetables (including egg salads with diet mayonnaise). She eats at least a half-dozen eggs every day. Her latest carbing-up discovery is Carboplex, a rice-flour derivative that really works.

If she ever eats junk foods, she will have only small amounts. For example, she may occasionally have a small amount of chocolate ice cream. She never eats huge amounts of food, knowing that moderation is the key to success.

Don Ross and Kent Kuehn help Kay with hack squats.

Kay Baxter has a legion of noisy fans at every bodybuilding show, invariably more than anyone else. As she moves from one dynamic pose to another with that famous grin, it's easy to see why.

Kay Baxter's Diet

4:45 A.M.

Perrier water
  with citrus juice
10 amino acid capsules
Vitamins C, B complex
Multi-mineral liquid
Kelp tablet

7:45 A.M.

Egg salad on pita bread
  (4 egg whites, 2 yolks,
  1 Tbs. diet mayonnaise)
Lettuce and sprouts
Perrier water

12:30 P.M.

Turkey on pita bread
Lettuce and sprouts
  or
Chicken and broccoli

2:00 P.M.

10 amino acid capsules
Fruit (melon or
  strawberries)

5:00 P.M.

Raw vegetable salad
Diet dressing

8:00 P.M.

5 oz. (150 g) broiled
  steak or fish
Baked potato (plain)
Steamed vegetables
Fresh fruit

Supplements

Vitamin A*
Vitamin B$_{12}$*†
B complex*†
Vitamin C*†
Vitamin E*†
Multi-mineral*†
Folic acid*
Potassium*
Calcium*
Chromium*
Selenium*†
Kelp*†
Zinc*
Dimethyl Glycine*†
Choline†
Inositol†
Methionine†
Amino acid (free form—20 minutes
  before meals)
*Breakfast and lunch
†Dinner

Notes

When eating a protein meal, Kay takes
one tablet of Hydrozyme, which contains hydrochloric acid to aid digestion.
Incidentally, Kay is a distributor for the
amino acids she recommends, which are
helpful for dieting when you want to re-
tain muscle size. Contact her at: P.O.
Box 746, Venice, CA 90291.

Kay Baxter's Routine

Precontest

5:30 A.M.

LEG WORKOUT	Sets	Reps		Pounds
Stationary Bicycle	1 (30 minutes)			
Leg Press	4	× 8–10	×	400–600
Leg Extension	5	× 15	×	50–80
Standing Calf Raise	5	× 20	×	460

8:30 A.M.

LEG WORKOUT		
Leg Extension	4	× 15
Hack Squat	4	× 12
Front Squat (Smith machine)	4	× 12
Standing Calf Raise	4	× 20
Seated Calf Raise	4	× 20

10:30 A.M.

MARTIAL ARTS WORKOUT
Stretching (30 minutes)
Calisthenics (15 minutes)
Hand-to-hand techniques (30 minutes)
Sword-handling techniques (40 minutes)

5:00 P.M.

Posing practice, dance class, or kick-boxing lesson

Kay Baxter

Training Workout

CHEST & BACK	Sets	Reps	Pounds	SHOULDERS & ARMS	Sets	Reps	Pounds
Incline Press (barbell)	5 ×	10–12 ×	Up to 155	Seated Barbell Press	5 ×	10–12	
Flye (flat bench)	5 ×	10–12 ×	Up to 40	Front and Back Press or	5 ×	10–12	
Pec-Deck Flye	4 ×	12–15		Seated Barbell Press	5 ×	10–12 ×	Up to 45
Cable Crossover	4 ×	12–15					
Chin	5 ×	8–10		Side Lateral	5 ×	10–12 ×	Up to 20
Pulldown (front)	5 ×	8–10 ×	Up to 140	Rear Lateral	5 ×	10–12 ×	Up to 25
Pulldown (back)	5 ×	8–10 ×	Up to 100	Upright Pulley Row	5 ×	10–12	
Seated Row	5 ×	8–10 ×	Up to 140				

Kay does thigh curls with an assist from Kent Kuehn.

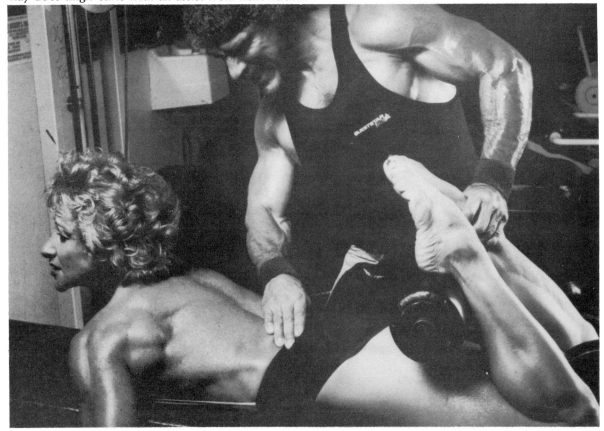

TRICEPS	Sets Reps	Pounds
Dip	5 × 10	
Triceps Pressdown	5 × 10–12	
Two-arm Dumbbell Extension	5 × 10–12	

BICEPS		
Incline Dumbbell Curl	5 × 10–12 ×	Up to 30
Preacher Curl	5 × 10–12 ×	Up to 50
Standing Barbell Curl	5 × 10–12	

ABDOMINALS

Kay does abdominal training at the end of each workout, starting with a circuit that she learned from Don Ross. Kay does the following exercises three to four times:

	Sets Reps
Roll and Tuck	1 × 20
Flutter Kick	1 × 20
Crunch	1 × 20
Jackknife	1 × 20

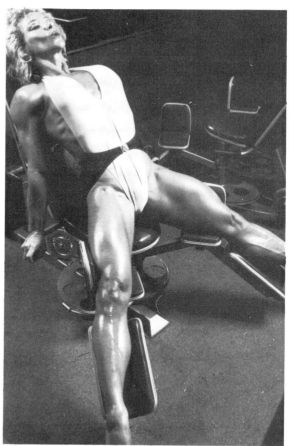

The scissors exercise works Kay's outer thighs.

Kay trims her midsection with seated knee raises.

In addition to the abdominal routine, she uses the crunch machine at Gold's Gym and also does twists with a stick for the flexibility benefits. Kay's sword-handling exercises also improve her waistline definition. Kick-boxing helps make her conscious of holding her midsection isometrically tight.

Kay Baxter is an advocate of regular massage therapy, which includes deep-tissue massage, hydrotherapy, and ultrasonic therapy as well as chiropractic adjustment. A number of well-known professional and amateur bodybuilders from Gold's and World's gyms receive this type of treatment to help heal minor strains and injuries that prevent them from training at their best.

JULIETTE BERGMAN

The Muscle Machine

O n November 30, 1958, in Vlaardingen, Holland, a perfect mould for a superior woman bodybuilder was born. Her name is Juliette Bergman. She is one-quarter Indonesian, Japanese, French, and Dutch.

After attending school in her hometown, which is located near Rotterdam, Juliette went to work as a secretary. At the time she was overweight and discontented with her physical condition. Then one day she and a girlfriend went to a gym to work out. After three months, Juliette's girlfriend had quit, but she was really enjoying herself and stayed with it. She made fairly good progress from the start, but she did have to diet as well to lose her excess fat.

It wasn't long before Ms. Bergman started entering competitions, and to her surprise she won the first contest she ever entered. It was the main Rotterdam-area contest, Ms. Rynmond. In 1984, she won the Dutch championships, the Grand Prix, and then the European championships in Madrid, Spain. Incredibly, she won a series of first places in every contest she entered. Then came the world championships in Brussels in 1985—again she was first. Turning professional, she went straight into the 1985 Ms. Olympia contest in New York City, her fifth contest of that year. However, the pressure of peaking for a fifth time was too hard on her, and she had difficulty in shedding subcutaneous fluid in her body. Her place was a disappointing fourteenth. She did, though, raise enor-

Juliette Bergman is an up-and-coming female bodybuilder.

mous speculation at her New York appearance. Her super potential was noticed by all.

Juliette just loves bodybuilding. Maybe that's why she competes so often. She even enters couples competitions with her partner Edward Boef. They have done many guest appearances in Europe with great success.

Currently, Juliette trains at Jim Lenszeld's Nautilus gymnasium in Middleharnis, near Rotterdam. But she doesn't use the Nautilus apparatus at all. She likes the free weights, and her body responds best to them. Nautilus is ideal for people who want to firm up and get fit, but it is not for the very advanced bodybuilder. Only free weights give her muscles mass and separation.

Juliette wins the 1985 IFBB Ms. Universe title.

Juliette Bergman

Forced reps are not part of Juliette's workout . . . at least not a big part. She uses them only occasionally on bench presses or seated pressing movements. Juliette said, "I like to exercise on my own if possible. Getting help makes completing a rep easier, not harder!" She does perform supersets, but only one day a week for her arms.

Juliette Bergman's mind-boggling proportions are truly amazing. Each muscle pops out from her frame. Her bones are not big. Her wrists, ankles, and knees are small and neat. Unlike most women, her calves are naturally huge. It may not seem possible, but it is true that she does not train her calves at all. She poses for photographers, demonstrating calf-training exercises, but she does not train her lower legs. Neither, incidentally, does she train her abdominals. (The only other bodybuilder who follows this same non-training pattern is Sweden's Inger Zetterqvist). Juliette is the only bodybuilder, male or female, who has correspondingly reduced her waist and built up her thighs to an equal 22-inch (56-cm) measurement! Now that's incredible!

Unlike most women bodybuilders, Juliette does not eat five or six times a day. In fact, she frequently misses lunch altogether. Her breakfast, however, is always substantial. One food category that she's not crazy about is vegetables. The only supplements she takes are Joe Weider's Anabolic Megapaks and potassium pills.

The day we interviewed Juliette Bergman was at the 1985 Ms. Olympia contest. The day after the show she had to train. She just did not want to miss a workout. At the Pumping Iron Gym in New York City, we observed Juliette's unbelievable shape. She trains with a pause between each repetition—super strict and super concentrated. The weights she handles are not light. For example, she half squats with 308 pounds and uses the whole stack of weights with the cables for many of her pulley exercises even though she's only 5 feet 2 inches tall.

After discovering that her waist and thigh had the same measurement, in accordance with the Grecian ideal, her neck, calves, and arms all measure the same 14½ inches (37 cm)! That's some accomplishment!

For those interested in contacting Ms. Bergman for seminars or guest posing (she speaks excellent English), she can be reached at: Nautilus Gym, Visserdijk 10, 3241 EC, Middelharnis, Holland.

Juliette Bergman

Juliette Bergman's Diet

8:00 A.M.

2 slices no-fat bread
  (made from eggs)
  with unsweetened jam
Granola, yogurt, banana
Coffee

1:00 P.M.

Protein drink with
  pineapple juice
Fruit

4:00 P.M.

2 slices no-fat bread

7:00 P.M.

2 grilled chicken breasts
Potatoes, pasta, or rice
Onions or green beans
1 glass of wine or Tia-Maria

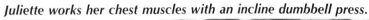

Juliette works her chest muscles with an incline dumbbell press.

—Juliette Bergman's Routine—

Frequency

Three days of training followed by one day of rest, then two days of training followed by one day of rest.

Split System

Monday: chest and biceps. Tuesday: back and triceps. Wednesday: shoulders and legs. Thursday: rest day. Friday: chest, back, and shoulders. Saturday: superset biceps and triceps. Sunday: rest day.

CHEST	Sets Reps	TRICEPS	Sets Reps
Bench Press	3 × 8	Single-arm Triceps Stretch	3 × 10
Incline Dumbbell Bench Press	3 × 8	Triceps Pushdown	3 × 8–10
		Lying Triceps Stretch	3 × 8
Cable Crossover	3 × 10	Single-Dumbbell Triceps Kickback	3 × 10
BICEPS			
Standing Barbell Curl	3 × 8	SHOULDERS	
Seated One-arm Dumbbell Curl	3 × 8	Smith Machine Press behind Neck	3 × 8
Incline Dumbbell Curl	3 × 8	Upright Row (narrow grip)	3 × 8
		Lateral Raise	3 × 10
BACK			
Wide-grip Chin behind Neck	3 × 10	LEGS	
		Squat (never full, flat feet)	3 × 8
Seated Long Cable Row	3 × 8	Leg Extension	3 × 8–10
Close-grip Lat Pulldown	3 × 8	Leg Curl	3 × 10
Single-arm Dumbbell Row	3 × 8	Hack Lift	3 × 8

Juliette Bergman

LYDIA CHENG

The Natural

Top female bodybuilders are extraordinary people, which is certainly the case with Lydia Cheng. She was born in the heart of New York City, lived there all her life, yet she speaks like a well-educated aristocrat. She went to the finest schools, yet almost took up the circus life, which would have led to an existence of constant upheaval and precarious living.

Lydia Cheng was born on May 20, 1962. Her mother is French-Canadian and her father, a former singer and actor, teaches voice. Lydia has three brothers, Philippe, Olivier, and Pascal, and one sister, Danielle. Her early life was spent in private school (St. Hilda's and St. Hugh's in New York City). From there she went to New York University where she obtained her bachelor's degree in French and economics. Lydia is soon to earn a master's degree in French.

How did it all start for Lydia Cheng? As a kid she loved to do gymnastics. She also did team sports. During her sixteenth summer, because of her superior athletic ability, she attended circus school, concentrating on floor acrobatics. One of the trapeze acts involved two women. Their show was billed as a "double trapeze act," and both women were extremely muscular. At an early age Lydia Cheng was aware of muscular women, even though, in reality, female bodybuilders were somewhat rare then.

Later on, while she was attending college, Lydia found herself without any physical outlet. Her studies gave her plenty of intellectual stimulation, but she

Lydia shows off her svelte physique.

craved some form of physical exertion. Her boyfriend at the time suggested that she try weight training. She did, and loved it from the start.

The schedule Lydia used at first was quite basic. It included the bench press, flat-bench flyes, pec-deck flyes, squats, lunges, leg extensions, curls, and triceps work.

Lydia Cheng

It was then that Lydia entered a few contests, the Ms. Apollo, placing fifth, and the Ms. Metropolis, where she garnered a third place. Ultimately, she won the "Big Apple," and then the Miss Tri-State.

"I'm really pleased that I was in at the beginning of bodybuilding for women. I loved doing the movie *Pumping Iron II—The Women*. But to come into the sport today can be very hard. The women are so ripped and defined. It's unbelievable! Many, though not all, take steroids. I'm known in the sport as a natural, and I don't mind reiterating here that I have never taken steroids and never will. I am totally against them," Lydia maintained.

Lydia Cheng is 5 feet 5 inches tall. She competes at around 132 pounds and seldom tops 140 between shows. There are so many opportunities in the media, films, videos, and commercials that she likes to keep in shape all-year round. She doesn't get fat between contests. Currently, she trains at the Pumping Iron Gym (2162 Broadway, NY, NY 10024), where she can be reached by anyone interested in contacting her for seminars or other commercial enterprises.

Ms. Cheng is not afraid to vent her views on any subject. She feels that drugs have brought harm to men's bodybuilding, and not until stringent drug-testing is done will the situation improve. She just does not see a true advantage in using chemicals to gain a so-called edge. Her personal view of bodybuilding is based upon a sincere love and positive enjoyment of training for health, strength, and shape. She never has to drum up inspiration to train.

"We mix up our training once in a while. When we get into the gym, we talk about what we are going to do. No body parts are left out. Bett Rubino, my training partner, and I get quite creative.

The important thing is that every part of every muscle is worked vigorously. We enjoy our training and frequently share a laugh. Actually, I think this is very important. We like to relax rather than remain tense during a workout. I believe the body rejuvenates quicker, and more oxygen is taken into the system. A sense of humor is vital," said Lydia.

On the subject of enjoyment, another of her loves is food, especially sushi, pasta with seafood, and Cajun and Indian food. She finds spicy foods delightful.

Of course, when it comes down to contest time, like any other top woman bodybuilder, Lydia forgets her favorites. It's all business. First the desserts go,

Lydia's double-biceps pose is a winner.

Lydia Cheng

then the fats. Eight weeks before competition she opts only for steamed vegetables, salads, fish, whole grains, and chicken. All the junk food is out.

Lydia's gym training is subject to a great deal of variance and alteration. She likes to pyramid her weights so that her joints are warmed up properly. Occasionally, if she feels a need to train hard, she will only use four reps in the squat and bench press to keep her muscles at peak strength. The degree of rest between sets is governed by the time it takes her partner to perform a set.

Lydia won fifth place in the 1984 Couples World Championships with Moses Maldonado. She credits Moses with teaching her a great deal about weight training, derived from his uncanny awareness of exercise form. A lot of his training perfection has rubbed off on Lydia.

One thing that confuses Lydia about bodybuilding is how to judge the female physique. She feels that the rules that govern the contest are too scanty. The present winning formula is too unrealistic for women to achieve naturally. She feels that symmetry and balance should count for a lot, but excessive vascularity is unattractive.

"It is not even attractive on the men. I think if the so-called standards keep on their present track, the sport will isolate itself. None of the classical sculptures showed the vascularity that is seen on today's bodybuilders," Ms. Cheng contended.

Today Lydia continues with her studies and is involved in one-on-one training with individual clients who require the service of a knowledgeable professional. Ultimately, she would like to write and teach at the university level. She's thinking of perhaps going into martial arts.

"One thing's for sure," she said. "I will always continue with my training. It's a part of my life now. There's no way I will give it up."

Lydia Cheng's Diet

Breakfast

3-egg omelet (only 1 yolk)
Mushrooms, scallions
2 slices whole-wheat toast
Coffee with skim milk

Mid-Morning Snack

¼ melon

Lunch

3½ oz. (105 g) tuna
1 slice whole-wheat bread
mushrooms, sprouts, tomatoes

Mid-Afternoon Snack

Apple or grapefruit

Dinner

Broiled fish (halibut or haddock)
  with lemon juice or vinegar
Steamed vegetables (eggplant or
  zucchini)
Glass of wine (occasionally)
Tea

Supplements

Amino acids (ornithine, glycine,
  tryptophane)
Desiccated liver capsule
Multi-vitamin/mineral tablet
Vitamin C
Enzyme tablets

Lydia Cheng

Lydia Cheng's Routine

Frequency
Six days a week.

Split System
Double split system (on an eight-day cycle, three days on, one day off.

For larger lat muscles, Lydia enjoys chinning.

Monday A.M.	Sets	Reps
ABDOMINALS	3 ×	15
Hanging Leg Raise	4 ×	15
Flat Leg Raise (weighted)	5 ×	20
Crunch		
CALVES	6 ×	15
Seated Calf Raise	6 ×	15
Leg-machine Toe Raise	4 ×	15
Donkey Calf Raise		

Monday P.M.	Sets	Reps
CHEST		
Incline Dumbbell Press	4 ×	10
Flat Dumbbell Flye	4 ×	10
Cable Crossover	3 ×	15

Tuesday A.M.	Sets	Reps
BACK & SHOULDERS		
Chin-up (to front)	3 ×	to failure
Wide-grip Pulldown (behind neck)	4 ×	10
Wide-grip Pulldown (front of neck)	4 ×	10
Low Pulley Row	4 ×	10
One-arm Dumbbell Row	4 ×	8
Straight-arm Pulldown	4 ×	8

Wednesday A.M.	Sets	Reps
BICEPS		
Barbell Curl	4 ×	10
Incline Dumbbell Curl	4 ×	8
Concentration Curl	4 ×	8
TRICEPS		
One-arm Triceps Extension	4 ×	8
Triceps Pressdown	4 ×	8
Dumbbell French Press	4 ×	10
Rope Pull	4 ×	10

Wednesday P.M.

LEGS	Sets Reps
Leg Extension	4 × 15
Squat	4 × 15
Leg Press	4 × 15
Leg Curl	4 × 15

Lydia performs a seated dumbbell press for her shoulders.

CAROLYN CHESHIRE

British Amazon

The year was 1979. The place was Lillie Road Fitness Centre in London. Twenty-four-year-old Carolyn Cheshire had crossed over from the basic fitness class, which she had thoroughly enjoyed for many months, to the weight room, which she found even more challenging. She had a seemingly uncontrollable urge to be stronger, fitter, and better muscled than anyone else.

"At first, people raised their eyebrows at the fact that I would even want to lift weights. I was put on a kind of circuit training whereby I would move from one exercise station to another. Certainly there were no movements like curls, shrugs, pullovers, or direct triceps exercises in the circuit. I was told that they would build ugly sloping shoulders, or else my arms would bulge unnaturally. As a successful model at the time, I went along with their ideas," Carolyn admitted.

Eventually, though, her craving to do several sets of each exercise was too strong. She was getting results. A close friend of hers designed a basic program that was the beginning of her hardcore bodybuilding career.

It wasn't easy for Carolyn. She got very little guidance with her weight training at the beginning. The instructor at her fitness club was of the old school, more interested in preserving Ms. Cheshire's feminine figure than catering to her lofty dreams of being solid from head to toe. When Carolyn trained, using multiple sets and high intensity, the instructor literally winced and

Carolyn Cheshire

showed his obvious displeasure. He did not want to be a part of her efforts to "masculinize her body." As her strength grew, it became more and more difficult to train effectively. Carolyn needed assistance on heavy flyes and dumbbell bench work. It became a job in itself getting the gym instructor to see her point of view. Only reluctantly did he aid her with her routine.

Born on July 23rd in the mid-fifties in Castle Donington, Leicestershire, Carolyn Cheshire was raised with three brothers, Timothy, Jeffrey, and Charles, and with one sister, Susan. She spent a happy childhood at the junior school in Castle Donington and then went on to the girls' grammar school, Ashby de la Zouch. She passed her "O" level (high school) and proceeded to attend the famed Loughborough College, where she obtained her diploma in business studies.

Her parents were very pleased when she took an avid interest in physical fitness. However, they were a little concerned when she got into heavy weight training. They wondered if the end results would be attractive. Perhaps she would strain herself, but now they are proud of her accomplishments. She calls it her "*magnificent obsession.*"

Actually, even Carolyn had doubts about the effects of weight training, at least in the early stages. One day, after doing several heavy sets of leg presses on the Lillie Road multi-gym, Carolyn was almost bowled over by the sight of her bulging thighs. A cold sweat came over her and for the next six months she only did light leg extensions for her legs.

"Looking back, I believe that I overreacted. I was carrying some fat at the time and had just pumped my legs. I now regard my six months of light leg extensions as *lost* training time. Needless to say, today I enjoy regular heavy

Carolyn has incredible muscle definition. Check out her arms!

leg workouts, including squats and leg presses," Carolyn said.

A few local shows proved the testing ground for Carolyn's first contest experience. On a challenge she entered a NABBA contest in Britain and placed high in the competition. Then came Britain's biggest event, the annual NABBA Miss Bikini. She didn't enjoy the experience. While the other contestants paraded around on high heels, Carolyn did her best bodybuilding poses from the rostrum. The audience didn't react with much enthusiasm. They regarded the bikini contest as just light relief from the men's show. They couldn't take it seriously.

After that disappointing experience, Carolyn really trained to add muscle. Joe Weider's *Muscle & Fitness* magazine published a few pictures of well-muscled American women, and they became an inspiration to Ms. Cheshire. She qualified for the NABBA Miss Britain, and got great audience response to her developed muscles. Unfortunately, the officials did not see things in the same light. One of them told her that she was too muscular and that the women's shows were *not* physique events.

Instantly, Carolyn realized that to be judged fairly, she would have to compete in the United States. Her first contest there was the National Capital Bodybuilding contest and she placed third out of twenty-three entrants, which was a big thrill for her. Debra Diana was first.

Carolyn went on to compete in the first Ms. Olympia contest and has entered every one to date, eventually beating Debra Diana in the 1983 event. Since then she has progressively improved her

An across-bench dumbbell pullover is performed by Carolyn for chest development.

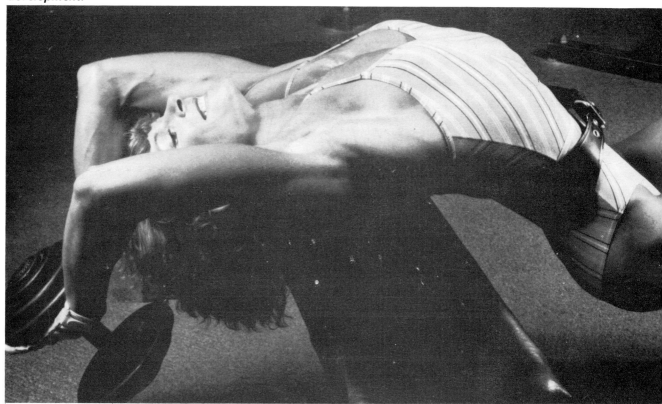

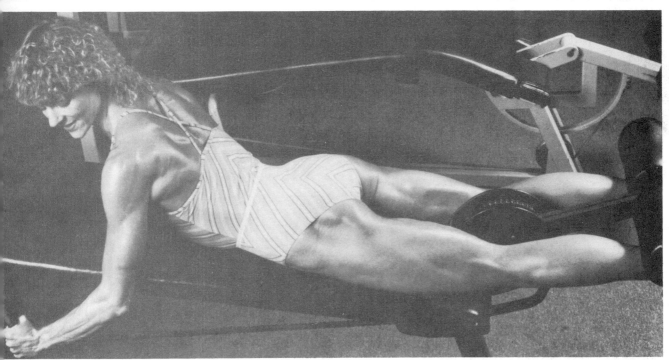

Carolyn squeezes out a leg curl for her thighs.

condition for every show. In 1984, she competed at 138 pounds, and the 1985 event in New York City saw her at 143 pounds. She maintains a fit 150–155 pounds when she's not competing.

Some of Carolyn's favorite foods include dried fruit, such as raisins, figs, and apricots. She enjoys good bread and admits to having a secret passion for Emmenthaler, Gruyère, and English cheddar cheeses, but she only eats it for a few weeks after a contest, or on very special occasions. Ice cream is another passion, but this is only indulged in for a week after a contest, at which time she also treats herself to biscuits, chocolate cake, cream, butter, and soft drinks. After two weeks it's back to basic, natural nutrition. She eats four or five times a day.

Carolyn now trains in the early morning. It's a new experience for her and she admits to being surprised at the amount of energy she has then. "The change of time gives my body a bit of a shock, but there are definite benefits to early morning training. There's a new atmosphere to the gym. It's quiet. I can concentrate fully surrounded by others who are equally as serious about their training as I am. It's delightful," she confessed.

Like many competitive professionals, Carolyn varies her routine occasionally. She currently trains on a six-day-per-week schedule, exercising two body parts per day (both at her early morning session). She prefers 10–12 reps for torso and arms and 12–15 reps for legs, waist, and hips. On basic exercises, like squats and bench presses, she pyramids her weights, adding poundage each set and lowering the reps accordingly.

Forced reps play a big part in her training. She likes to work with a training partner, invariably a male. For many exercises, she performs negative reps in addition to forced reps. If a training partner isn't available, Carolyn will cheat for a few reps at the end of a set. But she will cheat only when she can do no more strict reps. Only rarely does Carolyn stray from the straight sets principle, alternating a biceps exercise with a triceps movement (supersets) or reducing the rest between flyes and bench presses (the pre-exhaust technique).

Who has helped Carolyn Cheshire in her career? Julien Feinstein, Martin Alamango, Angelito Lesta, Andrew Searle, Eugene Cooney, Bill Dobbins, Robert Kennedy, and her present trainer Jim Lewis. She always has an ear open for new information. Frank Zane and Mike Mentzer have both given her some super tips. She reads *Muscle & Fitness*, *Muscle Mag International*, *Flex*, *Body Power*, and *Muscle and Co.*

Carolyn told us, "I'm learning all the time. I just adopt what I think worthwhile and discard what I don't think can help me. Most importantly, I am always willing to learn more, even though Bob Kennedy has said on more than one occasion that I know more about contest preparation than anyone else!"

As well as appearing in numerous films, including many of the James Bond pictures (some people believe she has the best-looking legs in Britain), and countless TV specials, Carolyn has also found time to write her own book, entitled *Body Chic* (Pelham Books, Bedford Sq., London).

Although Carolyn is trying to build herself up as big as her frame and genetic factors will allow, she is still very concerned about proportion and aesthetic line. "I think that those women who are physically big to start with, and who then take large amounts of steroids to get even bigger, are on a wrong course. Not even the men should go for size just for the sake of it. As for women, it is just not consistent with ideal womanhood. I am all for Amazonian size, strength, and super fitness for women, but I don't like bulky, unrefined bodies,

Carolyn Cheshire

where the quality of the physique has been destroyed by excessive steroid abuse. The limit for me is Corinna Everson. She has beautifully built legs, wide shoulders, and neat joints. And above all, she is charming and feminine as well," Ms. Cheshire pointed out.

Today Carolyn sees bodybuilding as a great spectacle. She still enjoys watching the men compete, especially if the posing is good. She would like to see bodybuilding in the Olympics, since there is no doubt in her mind that it is a sport, rather than an exhibition.

Carolyn finds it easy to discipline herself to stick with her training. She makes a plan, sets a realistic goal or contest date, and steadily treks onwards.

"I like to feel fit. That's my primary reason for training. It's like money in the bank. You can't take that away. Even if I stop training tomorrow, I will have done something positive for my body and general well-being. My long-term goal is to turn my interest in bodybuilding into my life's work. I want to stay with the sport in some aspect, make my living from it," Carolyn Cheshire said with conviction. For Carolyn, the hardest time is the last week prior to a contest. So many things can go wrong. You have to maintain size and improve definition, rehearse the posing routine, and watch food and liquid intake right down to the last calorie. The easy part is the actual training!

Ms. Cheshire puts the lat machine to good use.

—Carolyn Cheshire's Diet—

Carolyn Cheshire

Breakfast

1 orange
Oatmeal with raisins
2 broiled chicken breasts
2 slices whole-wheat bread
Coffee (black)

Mid-Morning Snack

1 apple
½ cup cottage cheese
2 slices whole-wheat bread
Coffee (black)

Lunch

¼ baked chicken
1 baked potato
Grapes
Coffee (black)

Mid-Afternoon Snack

1 whole-wheat roll
½ cup cottage cheese

Dinner

Grilled fish, lean steak, or calf's liver
Tomatoes and fresh vegetables
    (cabbage, cauliflower, broccoli, or
    beans)
Fruit (pineapple, pear, peach, or grapes)
Coffee (black)

Supplements

Amino acids
Multi-mineral tablet
Vitamin B_6
Vitamin C
Vitamin D
Zinc

Carolyn Cheshire's Routine

Frequency

Three days of training, one day of rest.

Split System

Day one: chest and back; day two: legs; day three: shoulders, arms, and abdominals.

Day One

CHEST	Sets Reps
Flat Bench Press	4 × 10
Dumbbell Bench Press	4 × 10
Supine Flye	4 × 10
Dumbbell Pullovers (across bench)	4 × 10

BACK	
Wide-grip Chins	3 × 10
Narrow-grip Chin	3 × 10
Pulldown (front of neck)	4 × 10
Pulldown (behind neck)	4 × 10
Close-grip Pulldown	3 × 10
Long Cable Row	4 × 10
Bent-over Barbell Row	4 × 10
Single-arm Row	3 × 10

Day Two

LEGS	
Squat (various foot positions)	5–7 × 15
Leg Press	5 × 15
Leg Extension	4 × 15
Stiff-legged Deadlift (from bench)	4 × 10
Leg Curl (forced reps)	4 × 10
Toe Raise (leg press machine)	10 × 20

Day Three

SHOULDERS	Sets Reps
Barbell Press	5 × 10
Barbell Front Raise	3 × 10
Lateral Raise	3 × 10
Bent-over Flye (face down on bench)	3 × 10
Upright Row	4 × 10
Heavy Dumbbell Shrug	3 × 10

BICEPS	
Wide-grip Barbell Curl	4 × 10
Reverse-grip Curl	4 × 10
Concentration Curl	3 × 10

TRICEPS	
Close-grip Bench Press	5 × 10
Lying Triceps Extension (straight bar)	4 × 10
Pressdown	4 × 10
Cable Kickback	3 × 10

ABDOMINALS	
Leg Raise (weighted)	3 × 30
Incline Sit-up (weighted)	3 × 20

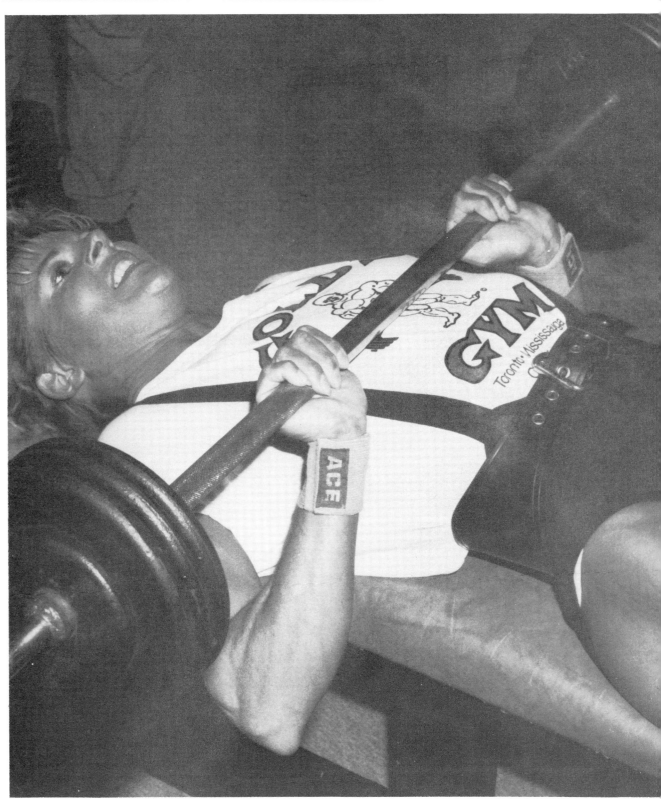

The close-grip bench press works Carolyn's triceps muscles.

LYNN CONKWRIGHT

The Tireless Competitor

"I was just crazy about gymnastics, and there was this one movement on the uneven bars called a Stalder that I couldn't master. My coach told me that I needed more strength to achieve it, so I took up weight training. I worked every single muscle in my body, including my hands and feet. Pretty soon, without knowing it, I was training exactly like a bodybuilder . . . and this was back in 1972," Lynn Conkwright said in an interview.

Not only did Lynn Conkwright learn the Stalder movement, but, thanks to her weight training, she became an all-round state champ. After that, when bodybuilding for women became fashionable in 1979, she was ready to compete. She took top place in the Ms. Virginia show, her first contest, at which she weighed only 98 pounds (she's five feet tall). Today she competes at 110. She went on to win the 1981 Couples World Championships and overall Women's World Championships.

Lynn was born on May 30, 1954, in Virginia Beach, Virginia. She has one brother, Bill, and two sisters, Shirley and Mary. When she was twenty-four she adopted a fourteen-year-old girl, Ann, who at eighteen had her own child. Lynn ended up being a mother to them both, but she always kept up her interest in exercise.

Lynn went to school at the First Colonial High School in Virginia Beach, and attended the Virginia Polytechnic Institute and state university. She started on the architectural program, but changed to exercise physiology. After

Lynn does an unusual pose on the beach.

Lynn Conkwright

graduation, she taught physical education at the very same high school that she had attended as a girl.

Her first workouts at the university gym were long because she didn't want to overlook any muscles. Lynn did basic exercises and isolation movements. She stretched for flexibility, practiced aerobics, and still found many hours each week to practice gymnastics.

Currently, Lynn Conkwright trains at six o'clock every morning. Her training partner is George Butts, former star of the Washington Redskins football team. He's a great training partner because he encourages her to push to the limit in her workouts. Lynn owns the Olympia Gym at 2250 Seashore Shoppes in Virginia Beach, and plans to open a similar establishment on the beachfront in the same town.

A few years ago, the famed tennis pro Martina Navratilova came to Lynn for advice. Lynn said, "I ended up training her. We gave her all the basics and designed specific exercises to even out her strength in both arms. We also came up with specialized cable movements to help strengthen the forehand, backhand, and overhand tennis strokes. It wasn't long after that that she won her first U.S. Open."

According to Lynn, Martina is a totally dedicated trainer, a natural who is willing to work. When the tennis star had moved to Florida, she arranged for Lynn to send some gym equipment so she could continue her training in her new home.

People who have helped Lynn Conkwright with her career as a bodybuilder include Steve Steinhilber, a close friend who owns the aerobics studio next door to her gym, and John Wareing (of Wareings' Gym). John got her started in weight training. Then his sons, Mike and Bob, helped her train. This was back

Leg raises help define Lynn's abdominal muscles.

Lynn uses a wall to maximize the effect of her stretches.

in the days before co-ed gyms, but they always let her train on men's nights. Two other inspirations to Lynn have been pro bodybuilders Chris Dickerson and Bill Pearl.

In agreement with most of the female bodybuilders interviewed in this book, Lynn is very against steroid use. She said, "To my mind, a champion woman bodybuilder is a person who has perfected her muscles for her body frame. What I hate is the thought of women taking steroids. I'm so fussy about drugs and chemicals. Right now, I have my business, I enter the Ms. Olympia *every* year, and I coach gymnastics. I just cannot get my life out of balance by doing a foolish thing like taking steroids.

I feel sorry for those women who have been talked into taking them. Besides, one day I want to have children and I wouldn't do anything to jeopardize their health. Even today scientists do not have all the answers with regard to childbirth and steroids."

Not only is she extremely busy, but there's a great deal of hard work in Lynn's daily life. Training for her has always been an adventure. She trains very intensively, using forced and negative reps. She does loads of supersets, but not in the conventional way of alternating sets of exercises for opposing muscles. Lynn works two exercises for the same muscle group. For example, she will alternate two biceps exercises, or two shoulder exercises. When she does exercise, each movement is performed with exaggerated slowness until she can't do another rep, after which she pauses for ten seconds and then performs one last one. The off season is a different matter. Then she usually does straight sets for everything.

Lynn doesn't have to motivate herself to train. She commented, "I've been competing so long. I was a cheerleader, gymnast, surfer, swimmer . . . you name it. My daily workouts are part of my life. It's natural. The only time I miss workouts is when I go on vacation. At that time, I don't even think about weights. But back in my gym, I'm attacking the weights with a renewed enthusiasm, always training for balance. I see myself as an extreme advocate of proportion and symmetry."

As far as her eating habits are concerned, Lynn enjoys tuna steaks, dolphin, swordfish, oysters, and clams, and she also loves sushi. Her supplementation program includes a daily multi-vitamin tablet. But prior to a contest (the last month), she takes amino acids. Only occasionally will she eat junk food, but never anything sweet. She just doesn't have a sweet tooth. But, of course, she stops eating junk food completely when she is training for a show.

Lynn Conkwright is very committed to the bodybuilding way of life. She has never missed entering the Ms. Olympia contest, and would love to win it someday. She said, "Bodybuilding is a sport within our hearts, but it is an exhibition in reality. It is still so young and there are numerous directions in which it could go."

—Lynn Conkwright's Diet—

Breakfast

Fresh fruit salad
Coffee

Lunch

Turkey or chicken salad
2 slices bread
Coffee

Dinner

Seafood or chicken
Baked potato
Green beans or sprouts

Late Evening Snack

Popcorn (occasionally)

Lynn Conkwright's Routine

Frequency

Three days of training, one day of rest.

Split System

Splits routine into three equal parts, one section each training day.

Lynn Conkwright

Lynn Conkwright

CHEST	Sets Reps
Incline Bench Press	3–5 × 8–12
Incline Flye	3 × 10
Pec-Deck Crunch	3 × 12
Pulley Crossover	3 × 12
SHOULDERS	
Press behind Neck	4 × 8–10
Upright Row	3 × 10–12
Dumbbell Lateral Raise	3 × 10
Dumbbell Press	3 × 10
Bent-over Lateral	3 × 10–12
Shrug	3 × 8–10

BACK	Sets	Reps
Lat Pulldown (behind neck)	3 ×	10–12
Lat Pulldown (to front)	3 ×	10–12
Single-arm Row	3 ×	8–12
T-Bar Row	3 ×	8–10
Chin behind Neck	3 ×	10
Hyperextension	3 ×	10–15
Stiff-legged Deadlift	3 ×	10–12

LEGS	Sets	Reps
Squat	5 ×	8–12
Leg Press	4 ×	8–10
Hack Slide	3 ×	10–12
Leg Extension	3 ×	10–15
Leg Curl	3 ×	10–15
Standing Leg Curl	3 ×	12–15
Leg Cable Pull (four different angles)	2 ×	12–15

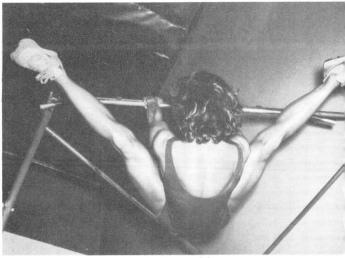

Lynn is an expert on the horizontal bar.

Lynn performs abdominal rope pulls.

CALVES	Sets	Reps
Seated Calf Raise	4 ×	12–15
Donkey Calf Raise (leg press machine)	4 ×	15
Calf Raise	4 ×	15

ABDOMINALS	Sets	Reps
Crunch	3 ×	12–15
Hanging Leg Raise	3 ×	10–15
Roman Chair Sit-up	3 ×	15–20
Twisting Bent-knee Sit-up	3 ×	15–20

BICEPS	Sets	Reps
Barbell Curl	3 ×	8–10
Alternate Dumbbell Curl	3 ×	8
Preacher Bench Curl	3 ×	8
Overhead Cable Curl (behind neck)	3 ×	8–12

TRICEPS	Sets	Reps
Close-grip Bench Press	3 ×	8
French Curl	3 ×	8
Pressdown	3 ×	10–12
Triceps Kickback	3 ×	10
Reverse Dip	3 ×	12–15
Parallel Bar Dip	3 ×	12–15

AEROBICS

Several times a week, Lynn runs, works out on the Olympic trampoline, or jumps rope.

CANDY CSENCSITS

Fitness Plus

Many women in this world would like to look like the scintillating Candy Csencsits . . . but it takes work.

In the late seventies, Candy was teaching physical education, doing plenty of exercise, running, taking ballet classes, all in an effort to control her weight. Yes, it worked, but she was still aware of her muscles not being completely toned. Then in 1980 the Ms. Olympia contest came to Philadelphia, and her husband, Frank, bought tickets. He was only moderately into weight training, but nevertheless, as physical-education specialists, they were curious about the then controversial subject of women's bodybuilding.

"I was absolutely in awe," said Candy, "when I saw those beautifully toned bodies. I just couldn't believe my eyes. I was immediately converted. Up until that time, I had used Frank's dumbbells a little . . . and he had me working out occasionally on the heavy (punching) bag. But I knew that from then on I wanted to take up hardcore bodybuilding."

Candy couldn't wait to get home and train after the contest. Her husband thought she would lose interest after a while, but she kept at it. She bought as many *Muscle & Fitness* magazines as she could find and subscribed to Doris Barrilleaux's *SPA* newsletter.

Actually, Candy's training program would change with every issue of *Muscle & Fitness*. She couldn't resist trying new techniques. She did, however, make

Candy poses at the beach.

very good progress the first six months. Then progress came to a standstill, and whatever she did, she couldn't gain or advance in any way. . . .

Candy Csencsits was born on December 29, 1955, in Northampton, Pennsylvania. After graduating from Northampton High School, she then went to college, where she got a bachelor's degree in health and physical education. Now she's working for a master's degree in nutrition.

Her parents took a dislike to bodybuilding when they saw Laura Coombes on television. Laura was far too muscular for their taste. And when they heard that Candy was bodybuilding, they were afraid she would masculinize her appearance. But now they're converted. Today even her mother trains with weights.

The nearest gym to where Candy and Frank live is 30 miles away, so naturally they have built their own home gym. After seeing that first Ms. Olympia contest, they kept adding equipment— plenty of free weights, benches, lat machine, thigh-curl and leg-extension apparatus. Everything was great until she stopped progressing. It was very real. There seemed no way out. Then she met Vince Fillipelli of the North American Gym, who put her through her first *real* workout. Candy had read about intensity

Candy does thigh extensions in her home gym.

but she didn't really understand it. She had achieved tone and enjoyed some initial muscle gains, but Vince showed her how to go that extra mile.

Before entering any shows, Candy observed them as a spectator. She was fascinated with how the women bodybuilders could project their personalities through their posing routines. She learned the compulsory poses and practiced her routine to music. Her former training in gymnastics and ballet was helpful.

Her first show was the New Jersey Classic and she surprised herself with a second-place finish. She entered dozens of shows until she realized that she couldn't hold peak condition from week to week. In 1981, she entered the Ms. Olympia contest and placed sixth. It was an incredible experience being up on stage with the idols that she'd been in awe of the year before. She only weighed 108 pounds.

Today Candy competes at 118 pounds, and only goes up by 5–8 pounds between contests. She said, "I just hate to let my weight get out of control. In fact, that's one of my pet peeves. I think that women who are only in shape one day a year do harm to the image of bodybuilding. What's the point of competing at 125 pounds, yet weighing 170 in the off season? I take pride in the way I look. I am happy to feel physically well. The rampant steroid use in the past got me down in the dumps, but I am happier knowing that steroid testing is under way. I'm so proud of Ben Weider's courageous landmark decision to test for them in 1985 . . . and consistently from then on."

In 1983, Candy won second place in the Ms. Olympia contest. Prior to that she had reached a plateau. A chance conversation with Anita Columbu ultimately led to her training with two-time

Candy Csencsits

What a pose!

Mr. Olympia Franco Columbu, who outlined a routine for her. Her contest training culminated with her moving to California to train personally with Franco for the last three weeks. Candy talked about it at length: "We trained at World's Gym, often in the sun. I really believe this helped. My skin became paper thin. Franco had me on loads of supplements including amino acids, which I had never really taken before. I also took loads of vitamins and fat burners. Franco had me on a very strict diet—high in protein, fish and poultry. The last month he even had me cut out grains and vegetables. To make up for a possibly unbalanced diet, I took more vitamins, especially B complex since I was having no grains."

Years ago, Candy Csencsits had a sweet tooth. Ice cream was a favorite food. Today she has no more urges for sweets. She likes white meats, fish, brown rice, vegetables, and fruits. She eats five small meals a day. The only dairy products she eats are low fat, such as skim milk, cottage cheese, or yogurt. She makes sure that she eats some high-protein food at every meal.

Candy's training frequency is built around the three-days-on, one-day-off principle. This is frequently used by top professional bodybuilders. On Mondays, she will train her shoulders, chest, and triceps; on Tuesdays, the back and biceps are worked; on Wednesdays, she attacks her thighs, hamstrings, and calves. Thursday is a rest day, and the cycle begins again on Friday. As a contest approaches, Candy will drop one rest day and train six days before stopping.

"My choice of repetitions depends on my goals," Candy explained. "If I want more size in an area, I will use 6–8 reps for that part only . . . while putting other areas on hold, training them with 10–12 reps. Right now I use forced reps

Candy works out some lat pulldowns on the pulley machine.

Candy Csencsits

on hamstrings only. I used to use them on leg extensions, but it hurt my knees and I had to stop. At contest time, especially when training with Franco, I exercise faster, as well as longer, even though I'm eating less calories. At that time we go pretty crazy, using supersets and giant sets."

As an IFBB official for women's bodybuilding, Candy wants to help the sport go into a positive direction. She would love to see everyone in America exercising with weights. She wants women to go for the max in bodybuilding, with two restrictions: firstly, drugs are strictly taboo, and, secondly, that muscle size be built with overall balance and proportion.

Candy elaborated, "There was a time when if you said you were against drugs, you were accused of being of the beauty pageant persuasion. Today, with the help of modern supplementation and aggressive training, women are getting built without drugs. You don't need them. Women taking testosterone makes about as much sense as men taking estrogen. It's crazy."

Candy's off-season training is still done at home. She trains alone—only occasionally will she ask her husband to give her some forced reps or spot her on an exercise. She used to work out in the early mornings, but currently she prefers night training. She doesn't miss workouts.

The most difficult part of bodybuilding is when she has to leave home to train in California. While she is grateful to Franco Columbu for his interest and personal help, she also misses her husband, Frank. She said, "He's so understanding. I really appreciate the way he wants me to get ahead. He stays behind and works while I train. It's hard on both of us . . . being apart, but it's only for those last few weeks before a competition."

Somewhere in Pennsylvania, a basement light is on. While the neighboring families sleep, a conscientious Candy Csencsits is churning out the reps, huffing and puffing her way through her exercises.

To contact Candy Csencsits for seminars or guest appearances, write to R.D.1, Box 726, Lenhartsville, PA 19534.

The squat exercise is one that Candy likes to pile on the weight.

Candy Csencsits's Diet

Off Season

Breakfast

Miso soup
Brown rice cereal
    or
Egg omelet with low-fat cottage cheese

Mid-Morning Snack

Nuts or seeds (optional)

Lunch

Tuna or salmon or tofu salad

Mid-Afternoon Snack

Nuts or seeds (optional)

Dinner

Fish or poultry or tofu
Brown rice
Vegetables

Supplements

Multiple vitamin tablet
Vitamin B complex
Vitamin C
Amino acids
Hydrochloric acid tablets
Calcium
Magnesium
Iron

Notes

*Don't eat at night.
*Don't eat sugar or processed junk foods.
*Eat low-fat/low-salt foods only.
*Drink lots of water.

Candy Csencsits's Routine

Frequency

Three consecutive days of training, one day of rest.

Split System

Day one: shoulders, chest, and triceps; day two: back and biceps; day three: thighs and calves. Exercise abdominals every day of training.

Seated calf raises are performed by Candy.

Day One

SHOULDERS

	Sets	Reps
Military Press	2 ×	8–10
Rear Deltoid Raise	4 ×	10–12
Side Lateral Raise	3 ×	10
Front Lateral Raise	2 ×	10

CHEST
Incline Press	4 ×	12/10/8/6
Incline Flye	3 ×	6–8
Crossover Flye	3 ×	10

TRICEPS
Cable Pulldown	3 ×	10–12
One-arm Reverse Pulldown	3 ×	10–12
Dumbbell Kickback	3 ×	10

Candy Csencsits

Candy warms up her muscles on the stationary bicycle.

Day Two

BACK

	Sets	Reps
Wide-grip Chin	6 ×	maximum
Wide-grip Pulldown	3 ×	8–10
Seated Row	3 ×	8–10
Bent-over Lateral Raise	2 ×	8–10

BICEPS
Alternate Dumbbell Curl	3 ×	8–10
Preacher Curl	3 ×	8–10
Concentration Curl	3 ×	8–10

Day Three

THIGHS

	Sets	Reps
Leg Extension	6 ×	20/15/10/8/6/20
Leg Curl	6 ×	20/15/10/8/6/20
Hack or Sissy Squat	3 ×	8–10
Butt Raise	3 ×	8–10

CALVES
Donkey Calf Raise	6 ×	maximum
Seated Calf Raise	2 ×	12–10

ABDOMINALS
Crunch	3 ×	maximum
Twist	3 ×	maximum
Leg Raise	3 ×	maximum

CARLA DUNLAP

The Competitive Edge

Could the sports-minded Carla Dunlap ever remember a time in her life when she wasn't taking part in some form of sports competition? It doesn't seem likely. . . .

Carla was born on October 22, 1954, in northern New Jersey, to a family of one brother, Warner, and four sisters, Alexis, Vanessa, Sharon, and Bobbi. After attending Newark Maple Avenue Elementary School, she went to Newark Arts High School where she majored in commercial art. Then she got a full scholarship to Newark School of Fine and Industrial Arts and majored in ad design. During her school years, she was a speed swimmer and competed in synchronized swimming. After she graduated she moved to San Antonio, Texas, and joined a synchronized swimming team, which won the Junior National Indoor Championships. In 1978, her team won the bronze medal at the newly created national sports competitions, and the following year they came in fourth.

Carla explained, "It was time to quit. But I didn't do it because we were failing to win. I did it because after twelve years of competing in water—winning state butterfly championships in 200 and 400 metres and individual medley—I began to *feel* the cold—literally. My top weight at the time was only 115 pounds and it seemed that at practice sessions, I was the first to really feel the cold. I would get the shivers when everyone else was quite normal."

Carla heads this lineup for the judges.

Carla Dunlap

Carla got into bodybuilding contests by sheer chance. Since she was the only black woman to qualify for swim events at the national level, this brought her to the attention of free-lance journalist Steve Wennerstrom, a former editor of *Women's Track & Field World* magazine.

Ms. Dunlap said: "Steve showed me pictures of Lisa Lyon and a few other top women bodybuilders. He told me about the upcoming Best in the World contest and encouraged me to enter. He even sponsored me. At the time I had done no body training at all. I competed as a swim-trained athlete and surprised myself by coming in fifth. Patsy Chapman, a beautiful black woman, won. Laura Coombes was at that contest. I had seen bigger women during the hundreds of swim meets I had attended, but never ones with such low body fat. I was caught up in the fascination of muscular beauty.

"When I met John Kemper, I was thrilled that he invited me to his gym. I didn't know how to train. When John realized that I was serious about bodybuilding, he said he would train with me. There's a great atmosphere at his Diamond Gym [732 Irvington Ave., Maplewood, NJ]."

When Carla's upper-middle-class parents heard that she had "discovered" bodybuilding, they soon got used to it. Carla's mother was a dancer, competing in dance competitions. Her father was very much the sportsman; he loved the outdoors, raising horses, and boating. Both encouraged and supported her and attended all her contests.

Training with Kemper was no picnic. Carla told us, "I never did get to start weight training at the beginning. I suppose everyone at the gym assumed I was tough because I had a well-defined swimmer's body. I did start progressing, but my legs were the weakest. Only now can I say that my legs are building up properly. At last I can squat with over 200

Carla Dunlap

A fine double-biceps pose by Carla.

pounds . . . but early on my tendons were so weak, it was an unrealized dream."

Weight training ultimately gave Carla Dunlap an additional ten pounds of muscle. She competes at around 125 pounds and is getting heavier each year. She's only five to eight pounds heavier in the off season. She feels her best condition was achieved at the 1982 Ms. Olympia contest, which she lost to Rachel McLish by one point.

When it comes to nutrition, Carla is always aware of her body weight, but that doesn't stop her from enjoying pizza or ice cream occasionally. She also loves sushi.

When she diets for a show she eats red meat, usually filet mignon, steamed lobster, chicken, turkey, tofu, natural grains, fruits, and vegetables. She always eats five or six times a day, but only occasionally eats large meals. She supplements her diet with a high-quality vitamin/mineral tablet.

Carla still swims five times a week, but she does it only to stay loose and flexible in the off season. When training for a contest, she reduces her swimming to three times a week and uses it as an aerobic exercise, to increase the metabolism and burn off any superfluous body fat.

The frequency of her routine is three days on, one day off, but if she feels low in energy or overtired, she will occasionally take two days' rest. She never trains more than three days in a row, not even at contest time. Her repetitions are usually between ten and twelve, but if she feels the need for strength, she will do six reps in some exercises, and alternatively do 15–20 reps at times when she feels she needs to pump the muscles. It's very much a body feedback situation.

Every exercise is done in strict form—no cheating. She tenses her muscles while she exercises them. Joe Weider noticed that the best bodybuilders invariably did this and coined the word "isotension." Carla also uses forced reps to finish a set. If she can only do six reps in the lat pulldown, for example, her partner will pull the pin in the weight stack and give less resistance.

Then she continues until she can't do any more.

She concedes that she has had lots of practical help from John and Shirley Kemper and from Phillip Kaan (son of the original superman, Mayo Kaan). Carla looks through *Muscle & Fitness*, especially because of the great pictures, but her main interest is reading about show reports on pro women's contests.

On the topic of femininity and women's bodybuilding, Carla voiced her opinions in the film *Pumping Iron II— The Women*, but she has more to say. As one who has *never* taken steroids, she nevertheless understands the athletic mentality: "I sympathize with the athletes who will let nothing stop them on their journey to the top. They are committed to use any tool they can. But I think that to play with genetics and hormones is potentially lethal."

Carla sees bodybuilding as a combination of sport and exhibition. She said, "You don't see the sport so much on stage, but the training is tough. I would like to see some form of strength feat brought into bodybuilding contests. I do appreciate all bodybuilders for their achievements. I know how hard they work to get all those muscles, but my personal preference in a man is for a more slender type of physique. I prefer the body of a dancer to that of a competitive bodybuilder. But that doesn't stop me from admiring the bodybuilder for his dedication.

"Before every event I have to plan and organize. I have to analyze. Now that I'm a pro bodybuilder, I am constantly having to change my routines— even choosing the right costume can be a headache. Whereas I love posing, now that I'm a pro, I have an obligation to the fans. In the old days I would just go out and wing it. Today I spend a lot of time choreographing every routine."

Carla Dunlap's Diet

Breakfast

Cereal with milk
3 eggs
2 slices whole-wheat bread
Herbal tea

Lunch

Tuna salad
1 piece of fruit

Dinner

Steak
Vegetable salad
Baked potato
Squash, broccoli, or cauliflower
    (steamed)
Herbal tea

Carla performs leg curls.

Carla Dunlap's Routine

Frequency

Three days of training followed by one day of rest.

Split System

Day one: back and shoulders; day two: legs, abdominals, and biceps; day three: chest and triceps.

Carla Dunlap

Day One

BACK

	Sets Pounds
Wide-grip Pulldown (Nautilus machine)	1 × 80
Close-grip Pulldown	4 × 90/100/110/120
Wide-grip Barbell Row	4 × 95/125–155
Bent-over Lateral Raise	4 × 30/45–60
Seated Barbell Row	4 × 110/120/110/90
Dumbbell Row	4 × 50/55/60/55
Deadlift	4 × 185/205/225/205
or	
Hyperextension	4 × 35–45

SHOULDERS

Shrug (dumbbell or barbell)	4 × 50 or 135
Military Press	4 × 80/90/80/70
Press behind Neck	2 × 80
Pec-deck Flye (facing machine)	4 × 40/50/60/50
Bilateral Raise	4 × 20/22/25/22
Dumbbell Front Raise	4 × 17/20/22/20
or	
Barbell Front Raise	4 × 30/35/35/30

WAIST

(also on day three)	Sets Pounds (Reps)
Seated Twist	3–4 × 50 reps
Crunch	3–4 × 50 reps

CALVES

Donkey Calf Raise (with 125-pound partner)	4 × maximum reps
Standing Toe Raise	2 × 260/280
Seated Calf Raise	8 × 80/90/110/90

Day Two

LEGS

	Sets Pounds (Reps)
Full Squat	4 × 135/155/175/175
Leg Extension	4 × 110/120/130/120
Single-leg Extension	2 × 40/50
Leg Curl	4 × 50 (lighter to finish set)
Single-leg Curl	2 × 20
Leg Curl	3 × 40/50/50
Stiff-legged Deadlift (bench)	2–3 × 135

BICEPS

Barbell Curl	4 × 55 (lighter to finish set)
Incline Dumbbell Curl	4 × 22/25/30/25
Reverse Curl	4 × 35 (lighter to finish set)
Cable Crunch	3–4 × 30

ABDOMINALS

Hanging Leg Raise	3–4 × 50 reps
Roman Chair Situp	3–4 × 50 reps

Day Three

CHEST

	Sets Pounds
Incline Barbell Press	4 × 95/105/115/125
Decline Dumbbell Press	4 × 40/45/50/55
or	
Wide-grip Bench Press	4 × 95/110/135/135
Pec-Deck Flye	4 × 50/70/80/70
Decline Pullover	4 × 50/55/60/65
Cable Crossover	3 × 30/35/40

TRICEPS

Close-grip Bench Press	4 × 80/90/100/90
Pulley Pressdown	2 × 35/40
Military Press (reverse grip)	4 × 45/55/ 55/45
Dumbbell Triceps Extension	4 × 35–45

CORINNA EVERSON

The Bodybuilder's Bodybuilder

Corinna has truly outstanding muscles.

Corinna Everson was born on January 4, 1960, in Racine, Wisconsin. She is 5 feet 8 inches tall and has two sisters, Charmaine and Cameo. From her earliest days, she was athletically inclined. Her parents have always been very conscious about good health and exercise. Her father was a gymnast and her mother was a track star.

While Corinna was in the sixth grade, her school coach told her parents that she should train for track. Later on, at Deerfield High School, Cory did work at track, but she had neither the fire nor ambition to go all out to win an Olympic gold medal. At the University of Wisconsin, where she studied interior design, she did continue with track and badminton, and was a campus star for four years in a row.

Ms. Everson said, "That is where I was first introduced to weight training. Jeff Everson was the strength-training coach at the university and he put me on a proper, balanced program. Prior to that, I had been doing silly movements like wrist curls and side bends. To tell you the truth, I hated weight training at first. We would do our stretching, then track training, and finally we had to hit the weights. It became a chore.

"I was always very muscular and fit, but when Jeff got me into a good weight program, I noticed some drastic changes. I got stronger and bigger. Soon I lost interest in track and became immersed in bodybuilding. After just two months, I had entered my first contest— the Ms. Mid America 1980. I won!"

Corinna weighed around 140 pounds the following year, but met with a setback. She was diagnosed as having a blood clot in her leg. She needed hospitalization and treatment, but made a strong comeback with Jeff as her partner by winning the 1981 IFBB couples championship. The two had fallen in love and were soon married. She went from one success to another. Finally, after competing for four years in a row, Cory achieved her dream of winning the AAU Ms. America contest in 1984. She then went

The reigning Ms. Olympia—Corinna Everson

Corinna shows amazing back definition.

on to win the IFBB Ms. Olympia contest in Montreal. Few other competitors challenged the decision. In fact, most of the other women in the contest agreed that Cory was a well-deserved and popular winner. This is a rarity in itself. Cory repeated her Ms. Olympia win in 1985 and was even more outstanding than ever.

Right now, Corinna weighs around 145–148 pounds in competition. She never goes more than eight pounds higher in the off season, in spite of having a penchant for pizza hamburgers, bagels, and Mexican and Chinese foods. She is very fond of tuna fish salad, especially with mayonnaise. She eats about five times a day and has recently discovered another favorite—oatmeal.

Why doesn't Cory Everson get overweight between contests? Because she trains like crazy, that's why! Cory explained, "People see me up there in a bikini posing to music, but they don't realize the brutal workouts I do to achieve my development. I have always trained extremely hard. I regard bodybuilding as a sport because I came to it via track and field. In fact, my training got more intense when I decided that bodybuilding would take precedence. I have never trained harder in any sport. I know I am fitter, stronger, and have better mobility than most other athletes.

"My husband Jeff designs my workouts and the routine is always changing. One week I'll do straight sets, then it'll be supersets, or giant sets, etc. I use assisted reps in some exercises, but never in rows, squats, or bench press. I have an injured shoulder, so I never force the reps too hard in the bench press."

Corinna doesn't do less than 8–10 reps for an exercise and in some cases she'll use 20–30 reps if she feels the need for added stimulation. On certain body parts, she will use an incredible 30–35 sets when training especially for a contest. After a workout, Cory is invariably overheated. She prefers to dress warmly for a workout so that she never gets chilled. Warm muscles work better.

Cory likes to use the pyramid system in most of the basic exercises. Here's an example of how she performs the squat exercise in her leg workout: 20 reps with 95 pounds, 15 reps with 115 pounds, 15 reps with 185 pounds, 15 reps with 205 pounds, 10 reps with 225 pounds (plus two more lighter sets to

Corinna does bent-over flyes for her rear deltoid muscles.

The hack machine is a favorite exercise with Ms. Everson.

finish). Incidentally, Cory's best performance is a whopping 275 pounds for 15 reps!

Even in the off season she works out twice a day. And before the Ms. Olympia contest, she trains three or four times a day, often putting in a total of six hours. (Two gym workouts, plus one hour on the stationary bike, and then another evening workout at home including posing practice.)

Cory told us: "I love to train but sometimes I get a little impatient before a show. It seems like I get a zillion phone calls, all by well-meaning friends, but at times it just gets too much. After my workouts I just want to put my feet up and relax. I start to get a little nervous the last couple of weeks prior to competing. Jeff and I have very private lives. Sometimes I wish I had time for other things. I would love to take tennis lessons and learn the piano. One day I will."

Those who wish to contact Cory for guess appearances can reach her at: Samson and Delilah Enterprises, P.O. Box 208, 7324 Reseda Blvd., Reseda, CA 91335.

Corinna Everson's Diet

Breakfast

Bowl of oatmeal
6 eggs (only 3 yolks)
Protein drink
  (100-percent egg whites)

Lunch

Tuna fish salad
Bagel

Mid-Afternoon Snack

Piece of fruit
Protein drink
  (100-percent egg whites)

Dinner

Tuna fish salad or chicken

Evening Snack

Bowl of oatmeal

Corinna shows how to do a dumbbell press.

This double-biceps pose is a show-stopper.

Frequency

Three days of training, one day of rest.

Split System

Day one: chest and shoulders; day two: legs and abdominals; day three: back, arms, and abdominals. Corinna does a lot of stationary bike work and posing and stretching in addition to her workouts. Also, her number of sets may go up to 30 or more per body part when training for a contest.

Corinna Everson

Day One

CHEST	Sets Reps
Bench Press	1 × 15
	1 × 10
	5 × 3–12
Incline Bench Press	4 × 6–8
Pec-Deck Flye	3 × 10–12
Cable Crossover	3 × 10–15
SHOULDERS	
Press behind Neck	4 × 6–8
Lateral Raise	4 × 8–12
Rear Raise	4 × 8–12

Day Two

THIGHS	
Lunge	4–5 × 12–15
Leg Extension	4 × 12–15
Leg Curl	4 × 12–15
Squat	7 × 10–20
CALVES	
Standing Raise	3 × 20
Seated Raise	3 × 20
ABDOMINALS	
Crunch	3 × maximum
Leg Raise	3 × maximum
Leg-up	3 × maximum

Day Three

BACK	
Lat Pulldown	4 × 20/15/12/8
Dumbbell Row	4 × 10
Close-grip Pulldown to Chest	3 × 12
Long Pulley Row	3 × 12
ARMS	
Dumbbell Curl	5 × 12
Triceps Pushdown	4 × 8
Pulley Curl	3 × 12
Triceps Extension	3 × 12
ABDOMINALS (See day two)	

CLARE FURR

Friendly Determination

"I guess my parents will never understand my love for bodybuilding. They really think I'm crazy. To them, bodybuilding is a ridiculous pastime for a woman. But then, they opposed my interest in basketball and karate, both of which I excelled at. . . . I just couldn't win my folks over," confessed the determined Clare Furr.

Clare was born on May 21, 1957, in the town of Greenwood, Mississippi. She has one older brother, Jay. Her initial introduction to weight training came in 1974, while she was a student at Pascagoula High School. A friend of hers had some weight-lifting equipment on his front porch and after school a few of them used to have fun trying out their strength lifting weighs.

While attending Tulane University, studying chemical engineering, Clare developed a great interest in karate. Soon she realized that if she was ever going to get her black belt, then she had better build more upper-body strength. Her martial arts instructor was into weight training himself at the time. He was an ardent follower of champion bodybuilder Mike Mentzer, "Mr. Heavy Duty." When Clare explained that she wanted to develop more arm and torso strength to improve her karate, he designed a routine for her. It was all based on Mentzer's weight-training techniques, utilizing the pre-exhaust principle (training a specific muscle with an exercise followed by an isolation combination movement). Clare alternated sets of bent-over rowing with lat pulldowns. Then more sets of incline

Notice the muscle separation in Clare's thigh.

dumbbell presses were alternated with flat bench flyes, and the barbell-press-behind-neck exercise was alternated with side laterals. She worked her arms with barbell curls, triceps pushdowns, and triceps kickbacks. After each workout, Clare would run for a couple of miles. This routine was performed daily for a year.

Clare Furr achieved her black belt in karate, but she never had the same dedication once she had gotten it. The success of her achievement was gratifying but it heralded a new era. She was now a hardcore iron pumper. She started going to bodybuilding contests, then she got the urge to compete. Her new training began at Boyer Coe's gym, Body Masters Health Club, in Metairie, LA. Until this time, her progress had only been nominal. It was gaining momentum in 1981. The Crescent City Gym is where Clare currently trains. She has never trained at home because she prefers gyms.

Clare entered the Ms. Westbank contest, promoted by Jimmy Gaubert. She won it even though she only had two weeks to lose a few pounds for the contest. Clare went on to win several shows, culminating with her USA Championships win in the lightweight class and overall title. She beat Velma Buckles, Jan Tech, Dawn Marie Gnaegi, and other top names. She said, "I was so scared the night before the show that I almost went home. There were so many top women around that I was psyched out—totally. I felt so inadequate. When I won the following day, I literally didn't believe it."

At 5 feet 4½ inches, Clare Furr readily admits that she loves food. She eats up to eight or nine times a day. Between shows, she boosts her weight upwards by eating heartily. Because she bulks up

Clare does angled leg presses for her thighs.

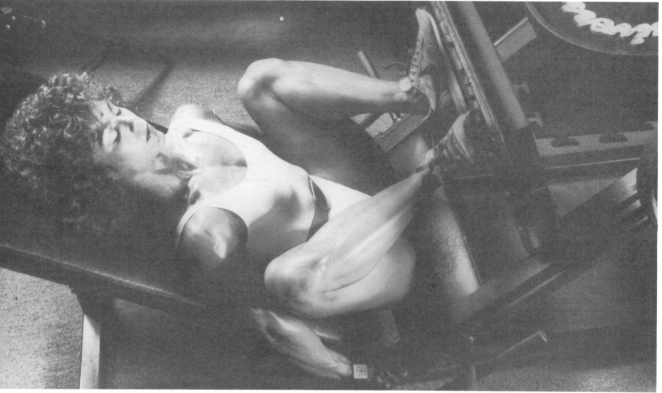

to 15–20 pounds above her competing weight, she has to start her diet four months before contest time. She gradually cuts out all her favorite foods to bring out her muscularity. But she hates the dieting part of bodybuilding.

And what are Clare's favorite foods? Pizza, cookies, cakes, noodles, pasta, beans, rice, and dairy products (especially Swiss cheese). She has no taste for red meats or chicken. She eats fish only occasionally, except during her pre-contest diet when seafood becomes her main nutrition.

For breakfast, Clare will usually have some cereal (Fibre One) with milk, but she doesn't drink milk by itself. She prefers to add milk or another drink to Weider's Dynamic Musclebuilder powder. It seems to work well for her, possibly because she doesn't eat too many protein foods.

At about 4:15 P.M. each day, Clare eats some fruit. At 4:30, she's ready for her training. She leaves the gym at 7:30. Her training frequency is three days on, one day off. Usually her first set of each exercise is done for high reps to warm up her muscles. Then she does between six and ten. She uses forced reps whenever possible, even on curls. The only exercise where she does *not* use forced reps is the single-arm dumbbell row. She usually pyramids the amount of weight for her exercises. She doesn't like starting out with heavy weights. Clare doesn't do supersets, and prefers straight sets.

Clare gives credit to her friend Steve Timmreck and to Jimmy Gaubert for her recent success. Gaubert taught her about using good exercise form, and he was a great help in teaching her how to pose in the early days.

The raging controversy over how *big* women should get is not a problem to Clare. She has a clear definition of what

Clare shows strict form in a heavy squat.

Clare Furr

is right for the sport. "I think a woman should get as big as she can as long as she maintains balance and symmetry. The point applies to men *and* women. When they get so big that the body loses balance, then the point of no return has been reached," Clare contended.

Is there much money in women's bodybuilding? Clare doesn't feel there is, at least not for most people. The idea has occurred to her to run a gym, but she concedes that the hours are long. Ideally she would like to be involved in bodybuilding or sports for the rest of her life. She has considered coaching. Clare

admires Gladys Portugues, who does lots of modelling work, and Rachel McLish. For the moment, though, she wants to do well in the Ms. Olympia . . . and then win it! Her best placing so far is fourth in 1985.

One of the things that really upsets Clare are the teenagers who take massive doses of drugs to help them gain muscle. She said, "I am glad that steroid testing is underway. It will legitimize bodybuilding as a sport. I just wish bodybuilding was as clear-cut as track and field, then we would have it in the Olympics for sure."

Clare Furr's Diet

Off-Season Diet

6:00 A.M.

Cereal (Fiber One or bran flakes)
with low-fat milk

9:30 A.M.

Banana bread
or
English muffin

12:30 P.M.

Tuna fish sandwich
or
Large baked potato
Frozen yogurt
Dried fruit and nut mix

2:30 P.M.

(Same as 9:30 A.M.)

8:30 P.M.

Homemade vegetable soup
French bread, pasta, or muffins
Cookies

Precontest Diet

6:00 A.M.

Cantaloupe
Low-fat cottage cheese

9:30 A.M.

Baked potato (plain)

12:30 P.M.

10 oz. (300 g) baked fish
or
Lean Cuisine
Baked potato

3:00 P.M.

2–3 peaches

8:30 P.M.

Protein drink (Weider's
Dynamic Musclebuilder)
Vegetable soup
Rice cakes
Cantaloupe
Low-fat cottage cheese

Clare performs abdominal crunches.

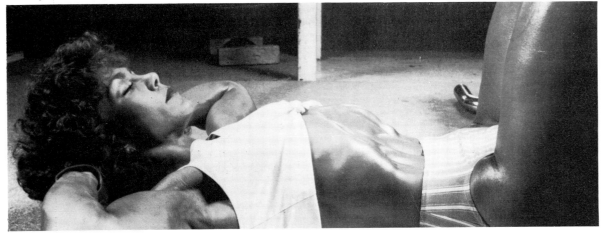

Clare Furr's Routine

Frequency

Three consecutive days of training, one day of rest.

Split System

Day one: abdominals, forearms, chest, back, calves; day two: thighs, shoulders, biceps; day three: abdominals, forearms, triceps, thighs, calves.

Day One—Afternoon

(45 minutes)

	Sets	Reps	Pounds
ABDOMINALS			
Hanging Leg Raise (weighted)	6	×6–10	
Bench "V" Leg Raise (weighted)	5	×6–10	
Crunch	1	×200	×10
Twisting Crunch	1	×100	
FOREARMS			
Wrist Curl (barbell)	8	×6–10	×65–75

Day One—Evening

(2½–3 hours)

	Sets	Reps	Pounds
CHEST			
Incline Bench Press	5	×6–10	×65/95/115/135/135
Decline Bench Press	4	×6–10	×115/125/135/135
Flat Dumbbell Press	3	×6–10	×50
Pec-Deck Flye	4	×6–10	×70–80
Dumbbell Pullover	3	×6–10	×55
BACK			
Chin (front)	4–5	×6–10	
Seated Cable Row	4	×6–10	×120/140/150/150
T-Bar Row or	3	×6–10	×160
Dumbbell Row	3	×6–10	×85/85/100
Bent-over Barbell Row	3	×6–10	×135
Deadlift or	4	×6–10	×185/235/265/265
Spinal Erector	4	×6–10	×70–80
CALVES			
Donkey Calf Raise	6	×6–10	
Toe Press	5	×6–10	

Day Two—Afternoon

LEG BICEPS	Sets	Reps	Pounds
Standing Leg Curl	6	×6–10	
Straight-legged Deadlift	3	×6–10 ×145	

Day Two—Evening

(2½–3-mile run)

SHOULDERS			
Standing Barbell Press	5	×6–10 ×55/75/85/95/95	
Wide-grip Upright Row	4	×6–10 ×75/85/85/95	
Dumbbell Side Lateral	4	×6–10 ×20/25/25/20	
Bent-over Lateral	5	×6–10 ×20–35	
Front Press (machine)	3	×6–10 ×90/100/110	
Close-grip Upright Row	3	×6–10 ×85–95	
Shrug	3	×6–10 ×165	

BICEPS			
Standing Barbell Curl	4	×6–10 ×55/75/85/85	
Dumbbell Concentration Curl	4	×6–10 ×25–30	
Preacher Bench Curl	4	×6–10 ×95	
Reverse Preacher Bench Curl	4	×6–10 ×55	
Reverse Wrist Curl	3	×6–10 ×45	

Day Three—Afternoon (Same as day one)

Day Three—Evening

TRICEPS	Sets	Reps	Pounds
Close-grip Bench Press	4	×6–10 ×95–115	
Lying Triceps Extension	4	×6–10 ×65	
Bench Dip (weighted)	4	×6–10 ×70	
Kickback or	3	×6–10 ×20–25	
Reverse Pushdown			

THIGHS			
Leg Extension	3	×6–10 ×80/90/100	
Hack Squat (machine)	4	×6–10 ×225/275/300/300	
Squat	4–5	×6–10 ×135/185/225/275	
Leg Press (45-degree angle)	3	×6–10 ×310/340/340	

CALVES			
Toe Press	6	×6–10	
Donkey Calf Raise	5	×6–10	

Day Four (2½–3-mile run)

SUE ANN MCKEAN

Staying in Touch

Sue Ann McKean has had an unusual upbringing. More than that, it was tragic. In the late sixties when the American military was in Laos, her father, a United States Marine, was shot down while he was flying in supplies to help the refugees of that country. His death had a traumatic effect on eighteen-year-old Sue Ann. She spent the next few years in looking desperately for something to believe in and stabilize her life. But the more she looked, the more she couldn't find what she was looking for. She attended a variety of schools and colleges, attempting to learn as much as she could, but something was missing in her life.

She was born in Oceanside, California, at Camp Penelton, to a family of three brothers, Mike, Scott, and Joe, and one sister, Sally. Sue Ann attended schools in Japan, Laos, Bangkok, and finally a variety of colleges in the United States. Among her studies were literature, biology, chemistry, anatomy, nutrition, and physics, but still she was aware of a void inside her.

Sue Ann recalled, "It was then that I discovered aikido [Japanese martial arts]. My previous urge to fill my head with facts lessened as my aikido training got into high gear. I got great satisfaction from training. Schools don't teach you how to deal with the trials and tribulations of life—how to connect with people—but I was getting this out of my martial arts lessons."

Sue Ann studied aikido until she earned a black belt. After that, she taught aikido at the California State Uni-

Sue Ann is a martial-arts devotee.

versity at Hayward, and at San Jose, the California Institute of Transpersonal Psychology, and also gave private lessons.

While training in 1981 she got kicked on the side of her leg, which caused a knee injury. Sue Ann refused to have an

What biceps!

operation. Her doctor accepted her decision but recommended that if she wanted to regain full use of her knee, she should consider weight training. She did leg extensions and leg curls daily. Soon she was doing additional exercises, which gave her extra energy. Prior to this, Sue Ann had not had many positive thoughts about bodybuilders, seeing them as narcissistic people.

The gym that Sue Ann trained at was called Family Fitness in Mountainview, California. It was a club competition that first got her to enter a bodybuilding contest. She had never seen one of any kind before but agreed to compete because her aikido teacher encouraged her to do it. Since she didn't know how to pose, she did aikido movements, and actually finished in fourth place. But more than that, she got hooked on bodybuilding!

Sue Ann read all the magazines on bodybuilding, but realized that she had a lot to learn about training, competing, and posing. Within three months of starting to bodybuild, she had won the Ms. San Jose title, and before a year's training was under her belt she had placed third in the "America," as it was then known.

Because of Sue Ann's muscular physique, people suspected that she was on steroids. She heard it time and time again. This was the price she was paying for being one of the most muscular women in America. She said, "I got so tired of being accused of being on steroids. I never was and never will be. I am not even tempted to try steroids. I regard them as cheating. Women use them to get a shortcut to fame. But I see them only as a shortcut to burn out."

Between January and September of 1983, Sue Ann McKean entered ten shows and she learned something at each, whether she won or not. She was proud to have won the Ms. California in

"Rugged" is the only word to describe Sue Ann's single-arm dumbbell row.

Sue Ann does a martial-arts pose.

1984. For that contest, she was in good shape and afterwards decided to only compete once or twice a year. Reaching a peak for a contest is pretty tough and it just can't be done too frequently. Sue Ann McKean is a realist. She doesn't have aspirations to win the Ms. Olympia—not yet, anyway. She likes to set small goals and achieve them one step at a time.

When it comes to tossing iron, Sue Ann really loves the challenge. She thrives on the workout itself. She doesn't use forced reps—and seldom trains with a partner. The key word to her training is "variety."

She described her training routine as follows: "I use some straight sets, but if the need for change is there, I will do supersets or trisets just for the sake of variation. Sometimes I superset chest and back exercises; I like that combina-

tion, as well as alternating biceps and triceps movements. For the first six months of my training, I worked out every day. I just couldn't stand to take a day off. Now I train three three days on, one day off, but I even change my frequency around if progress is slow. I like to feel the groove . . . then change."

Sue Ann pumps iron at Gold's Gym in San Jose, California, or the Gold's Gym in San Francisco. She has picked up knowledge from everywhere, and tunes in to her body's feedback system. She respects the advice of trainer Vince Gironda and bodybuilders Arnold Schwarzenegger, Scott Wilson, and Mark Riefkind. She reads most of the magazines including *Strength Training for Women*, *Flex*, *MuscleMag International*, and *Muscle & Fitness*. She said, "I never had a coach, but my aikido mentor, Robert Nadeau, has come closest to being one to me. He's a champion of women. He treats women as equal to men. I would never have entered a contest if it weren't for his encouragement. He taught me to embrace problems, to meet a challenge, and open myself up to new vistas."

Even though Sue Ann lives in the San Francisco area, she isn't a seafood devotee—she may go for six months without it. Then, if the urge presents itself, she will indulge in sushi. She prefers to eat meat. She doesn't eat junk foods, and follows her instincts by staying in touch with her body. The only time when she doesn't eat right is on those rare occasions when she's nervous or out of touch. But she soon gets back on track. If Sue Ann is dieting, she reduces her calories slowly. Since she never gets very fat, she doesn't have to make drastic dietary changes.

Sue Ann McKean is truly a dedicated bodybuilder. We will see a lot more of her on the contest circuit.

Sue Ann McKean's Diet

10:00 A.M.

3 slices sprouted toast
  with margarine
Banana
Coffee

3:00 P.M.

Chicken, turkey, or eggs
Potato, corn, or rice crackers

6:00 P.M.

Fruit, cookies, or bran muffin

11:00 P.M.

Chicken, turkey, hamburger,
  cottage cheese, or eggs
Vegetables or salad

1:00 A.M.

2 slices toast
1 glass of non-fat milk
  or cup of cocoa (hot)

Notes

Before her morning workout, Sue Ann takes three or four teaspoons of amino acids and a vitamin supplement. Her precontest diet varies from her off-season plan when she reduces her food intake by 500 calories from fats and dairy products. Before a contest, she eats more fruits and vegetables and protein (mostly in the form of amino acid supplements).

A press-behind-neck exercise performed by Sue Ann.

Sue Ann McKean's Routine

Frequency

Three consecutive days of training, one day of rest.

Split System

Day one: chest and back; day two: legs; day three: shoulders, triceps, biceps, and forearms. She trains her abdominals every day.

Sue Ann works her shoulders with upright rows.

Day One

CHEST	Sets	Reps
Incline Barbell Press	5 ×	15/12/10/8/6
Flat Dumbbell Bench Press	5 ×	15/12/10/8/6
Flyes (flat or Incline)	4 ×	12–15
Parallel Bar Dip	4 ×	12–15
Cable Crossover or Pec-Deck Flye	4 ×	12–15

BACK		
Chin-up (front, back, with various grips)	5 ×	8–12
Bent-over Row	4 ×	12/10/8/6
Pullover	4 ×	12/10/8/6
Cable Row	4 ×	10–12
Hyperextension	4 ×	15–25

Day Two

LEGS		
Leg Press (narrow foot position)	5 ×	15/12/10/8/15
Front Squat	5 ×	15/12/10/8/15
Leg Extension	3 ×	15
Lunge	4 ×	15
Leg Curl	4 ×	15/12/10/8
Seated Leg Curl	4 ×	12/10/8/6
Cable Kickback	4 ×	12/10/8/6

CALVES		
Donkey Calf Raise	5 ×	20–30
Standing Calf Raise	5 ×	20/15/12/10/8
Seated Calf Raise	5 ×	10–15

Day Three

DELTOIDS

Press behind Neck ⎤ Lateral Raise ⎬ 4 trisets × 12–15 Bent-over Lateral ⎦	

Arnold Press ⎤ Upright Row ⎬ 4 trisets × 12–15 One-arm Dumbbell ⎦ Raise	

TRICEPS

Pulley Pushdown	4 × 15/12/10/8
Standing Barbell Triceps Stretch	4 × 10–15
Rope Extension	4 × 10–15
Dumbbell Kickback	4 × 10–15

BICEPS

Incline Dumbbell Curl	3–4 × 15
Preacher Bench Curl	3–4 × 10–12
Hammer Curl	3–4 × 8–10
Concentration Curl	3–4 × 12–15

FOREARMS

Incline Wrist Curl	4 × 10–15
Barbell Roll-up (behind back)	4 × 10–15

ABDOMINALS

Crunch ⎤ Incline Sit-up ⎬ Rope Pulldown/ ⎬ 3 giant sets Crunch ⎬ Leg-up ⎦	

Thigh extensions develop Sue Ann's legs.

ERIKA MES

Magnetism and Muscles-

Ballet classes used to be Erika's first choice in physical activity. She had an abundance of energy and got instruction at a local school in Rotterdam, Holland. Although she didn't tell anyone, in her heart she wanted to be a star in some form of show business.

Attached to the main hall where Erika took her ballet lessons was a small, dingy weight room. Heavy dumbbells and barbells littered the floor. It didn't look inviting at first, but being inquisitive, Erika started using the weights at the end of 1979. Needless to say, after a few sessions, she was sore from head to toe, but there was more. She was getting stronger and more muscular, especially her legs. She ate heartily, gained size all over, and felt great about her training. She was on her way.

Erika Mes was born on November 13, 1961, in Rotterdam, Holland. She has one brother, Ruud, who bodybuilds for recreation. Her schooling was mainly at the Martin Luther High School, where she learned to speak French, German, and English, as well as Dutch, her native tongue.

After five months she gave up ballet. Although at first she only trained twice a week, she soon began working out three times a week. She said, "It was all so much fun. At shows, people seemed to like me, and in turn I wanted to please them. That's why I like posing so much—to entertain people. Even though my ambition is to one day win the IFBB Ms. Olympia, I do not feel that winning is everything. The audience—my fans—

Erika shows off her well-sculpted body lines.

Erika cycles for aerobic exercise in Holland.

are the ones I want to please. I like gaining new fans, too, at shows where the audience hasn't seen me before."

When Erika's folks found out that she was training with weights, they showed no particular interest. But when she won the Dutch Championships, her father became really proud and her mother attended every show she entered.

Erika works a long and hard day in the family business. Her parents own a small hotel in Rotterdam. She fits her training in at three in the afternoon because the gym is not crowded and there is a relaxed atmosphere. Her regular training partner is the Dutch world champion Berry DeMey. He's a good-natured man, has an active sense of humor, and is bigger than the Farnese Hercules. After trying every gym in town, Erika has settled on Body Shape, which is located at Spangesekade 21 in Rotterdam.

In her off season, she seldom weighs more than 124 pounds (at 5 feet 1 inch in height), and her weight drops to about 118 for a contest. Erika commented, "I never watch my weight. It's the appearance that counts. I just look in the mirror. I would like to be a little bigger overall, but it's the low body fat that is important to the judges. Invariably, I enter weighing under 120 pounds. Actually, I have so many guest-posing exhibitions throughout the year that I'm pretty well always in 90 percent shape."

Many fans have been won over because Erika's body shape is admired by both sexes of all ages. Most people agree that she has an ideal body for a female athlete. Her friendly face and beautiful smile must also have something to do with it.

After her string of wins with the WABBA organization, winning the 1980 World Championships in Paris, Erika got more and more interested in pure (hardcore) bodybuilding. The following year, again at the world championships, she kicked off her high-heel shoes and posed barefoot on the stage. It was a first in Europe where high-heel shoes were traditionally worn by women competitors. Her routine went over well enough to afford her second place to Jacqueline Nubret.

It wasn't long before Erika came to realize that the IFBB shows appeared to have a higher overall standard than any other organization. Always one to go for the top, she made the decision to switch associations. She would compete for the world women's title in London in 1983. She is most proud of this achievement because several people in Holland were declaring that she had no chance of doing well in the IFBB. Far from being hurt or discouraged by these remarks, Ms. Mes trained with a new enthusiasm, and she won the title.

Because of her high metabolism, Erika finds herself virtually eating all day long. She has at least six sit-down meals, two of which are quite large. Her favorite foods are bread, cheese, ice cream, and Indonesian food made with rice, lamb, and a wide assortment of vegetables. She also enjoys Italian food, particularly pizza and macaroni, and loves fruit of all kinds. Erika drinks no milk at all for the simple reason that she doesn't enjoy it.

At the conclusion of an important contest, there is a lull in her training. After a few weeks she returns to the gym, training her whole body three times a week without excessive effort, using only one exercise per body part. Gradually she works into training three times a week, two exercises per body part; then four times a week, working a split routine of three body parts per day (usually chest, back, and shoulders, or thighs, calves, and arms). She does ab-

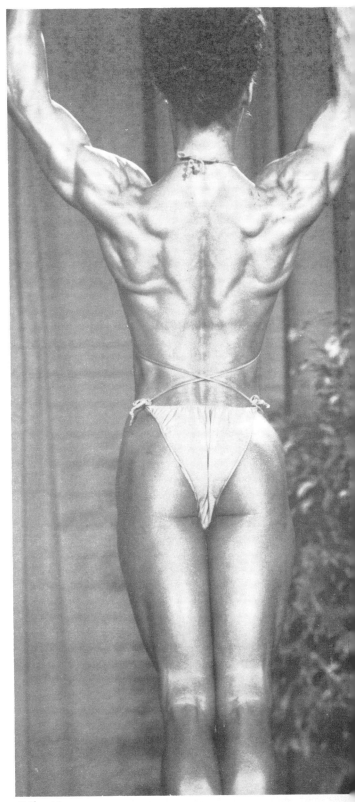

Erika Mes

dominal work once or twice a week. The usual frequency for this heavier training is two days on, one day off.

Like any enthusiastic bodybuilder, Erika periodically makes some changes and variations in her workouts. Currently, she is training with Dutch champ Paul Koole. She said, "We start off with low reps, very heavy, then as a contest comes along we take the reps up to about fifteen. Paul and I often perform descending reps (twelve, ten, eight, six, four) on the basic exercises during maintenance training."

She loves to do forced reps on most exercises, except those for her biceps, which she makes up for by curling in a very strict fashion, then really burning them out with cheat reps until she can

do no more. Occasionally, Erika will superset her arm exercises to shock them into a new growth pattern. Her usual rest time between sets is just as long as it takes her partner to do his set—about 30–40 seconds.

She commented, "We take longer rests between sets of squats because they are so demanding, and because I always wrap my knees. I unwrap them between sets to let the blood flow more easily. Right now I am squatting with 230 pounds, almost double my body weight.

"It works out well when I train with a top bodybuilder like Berry DeMey or Paul Koole, but I usually end up training with my boyfriend, Chris Bernaards, during the last few weeks. Because he knows the importance of a contest to

Erika does dumbbell lateral raises to build up her shoulder width.

Erika Mes and Berry DeMey

me, he will adjust his training totally to the pace that I need. I would neither want nor expect this from my other training partners, but Chris does it willingly because he wants me to be at my best."

Erika has learned many things from Berry DeMey. Interestingly, what works for his body invariably works for her. As an example, they cut their sodium (salt) intake out during the last two days before a show, whereas many contestants seem to cut it out eight or nine days prior.

Erika's ambition is to get more well known. She likes positive publicity and wants to do well in the Ms. Olympia contest, placing as high as she can.

Since she doesn't take any drugs to enhance her growth, she is against others who do. She feels they lose their feminine shapes. Erika admires Cory Everson's physique, believing that "she has everything."

One of the magazines that Erika enjoys reading is Joe Weider's *Sport & Fitness*. It has some good advice about nutrition. She also reads *Flex*, *MuscleMag International*, *Muscle & Fitness*, and the Dutch magazine *Fit*.

The hardest part of contest preparation for Erika Mes is starting to diet. She told us, "It always goes wrong. I make a decision to start on a certain day and end up cheating. Maybe it's because I have food all around me in the hotel. After a few days I'm settled in and everything runs according to plan. I do not cheat

Erika demonstrates alternate dumbbell raises.

Erika Mes

anymore. The results start to show, and I am encouraged more and more to keep to my diet. As my physique starts to look defined, I practice a few poses at home. I see bodybuilding first and foremost as a sport, but the contest itself as an art. That's why I put so much into my routine. Few people realize that bodybuilding training is so intense, but much work has to be put into the posing routine, too."

Erika is known for her dynamic free-posing routine. Frequently, the bodybuilding press has acknowledged that she is one of the most exciting posers to watch. At international contest level, this is high praise indeed.

"The funny thing is," said Erika, "although I pose now and again in front of the mirror at home, Chris and I never start putting the final routine together until the last couple of weeks. With our backs against the wall, there is tremendous pressure to be prepared for the contest deadline. I end up practicing all day long during those last few days. It's hectic. We go crazy but it all comes together in the end."

Erika Mes's Diet

Off Season

6:00 A.M.

2 eggs
2 slices brown bread
  with cheese
Coffee

10:00 A.M.

1 slice brown bread
Fruit

1:00 P.M.

Chicken with rice
Vegetables

4:00 P.M.

Protein drink

7:30 P.M.

Meat, fish, or chicken
Potato or rice
Vegetables
Fruit

Precontest

6:00 A.M.

3 egg whites
Fruit

8:00 A.M.

Cereal with banana

1:00 P.M.

Chicken or tuna fish (water packed)
Rice

2:00 P.M.

Fruit

4:00 P.M.

Protein drink with water

7:30 P.M.

Broiled fish or chicken with 2 egg whites
Potato or rice

10:00 P.M.

Protein drink with water

Notes

For the last weekend before a contest, Erika restricts her intake of carbohydrates. For the next four days, she goes back to her regular diet. On the last two days, she cuts out salt completely and loads up with high-carbohydrate foods (such as potato).

Erika takes delight in this enthusiastic pose.

Frequency

Three days of training followed by one day of rest.

Split System

Day one: chest and back; day two: legs and calves; day three: shoulders, arms, and abdominals.

Day One

CHEST	Sets	Reps	Pounds
Bench Press	1 ×	12	× 80
	2 ×	8	× 110
	1 ×	6	× 130
	1 ×	6	× 150
	1 ×	till failure	× 110
Incline Barbell Press	3 ×	10	× 110
	1 ×	15	× 86
or			
Flat Bench Dumbbell Press	3 ×	8–10	× 44
	1 ×	till failure	× 35
Standing Cable Crossover	2 ×	till failure	
BACK			
Wide-grip Chin	4 ×	till failure	
Close-grip Chin	4 ×	till failure	
Seated Cable Row (weighted)	4 ×	8–10	
Bent-over Row	2 ×	8	× 110
	2 ×	6	× 135
T-Bar Row	3 ×	8	× 110
Wide-grip Lat Pulldown	3 ×	12	
or			
Hyperextension	3 ×	till failure	

Day Three

SHOULDERS	Sets	Reps	Pounds
Press behind Neck	1 ×	15	× 45
	1 ×	12	× 75
	2 ×	8	× 90
	1 ×	6	× 110
Front Press (machine)	1 ×	10	*
	2 ×	8	*
	1 ×	6	*
Dumbbell Side Lateral	4 ×	8	× 30
One-arm Cable Lateral	4 ×	10–12	*
	4 ×	8–12	*
Shrug or Upright Row	4 ×	8–12	*
BICEPS			
Barbell Curl	1 ×	12	× 45
	1 ×	10	× 55
	2 ×	8	× 60
	1 ×	6	× 80
Alternate Dumbbell Curl	4 ×	8	× 23
Concentration Curl	4 ×	12	× 20
TRICEPS			
Pushdown (machine)	1 ×	12	× 50
	4 ×	10	× 70
French Press	1 ×	10	× 70
	3 ×	8	× 80
Dumbbell Extension (behind neck)	4 ×	till failure	× 22
Parallel Bar Dip	3 ×	till failure	

ABDOMINALS
Depending on her energy level, she trains her abs two to six times per week with a variety of crunches, sit-ups, and twists.

Day Two

LEGS	Sets	Reps	Pounds
Squat	1 ×	15	× 110
	1 ×	12	× 155
	1 ×	10	× 180
	1 ×	8	× 200
	1 ×	6	× 220
Hack Squat or	5 ×	10	× 80
Leg Press	1 ×	12	× 180
	1 ×	10	× 200
	1 ×	8	× 250
	1 ×	6	× 270
	1 ×	12	× 160
Leg Extension	4 ×	10–12	*
Leg Curl	4 ×	12–15	*
Standing Leg Curl	4 ×	10–15	*
Seated Calf Raise	4 ×	15–20	*
Standing Calf Raise	4 ×	15–20	*

Note: Before a contest she does lunges after her leg workout with a 40-pound barbell on her shoulders.

*as much weight as possible

LYNNE PIRIE

Dr. Lynne Pirie
Sports Medicine

Intelligence and Elegance.

She is everything that exemplifies success. It's more than appearance; there is an underlying calmness about her. Dr. Lynne Pirie is a nice person . . . with a dynamite body. On top of it all, she is incredibly disciplined and bright.

She was born in Cambridge, Canada (formerly known as Galt) on January 2, 1950. She has two brothers, Kenneth and David, and two sisters, Christine and Maureen, who all keep fit and healthy using weights. After attending Bradford Pauline Johnston High School, she went to the University of Western Ontario in London to study physical education (she got her master's degree in growth and motor development). Next stop was Michigan State University in East Lansing, where she worked on her Ph.D. in kinesiology and exercise physiology. Then she went to medical school at Michigan State to study at the college of Osteopathic medicine. She did her internship and residency in Phoenix, Arizona.

Today she lives in Phoenix permanently with her husband, John, and has her own practice, a sports medicine clinic at the North Phoenix Health Institute (750 E. Thunderbird Road, Suite 4). When complimented on her obvious success, Lynne concedes that she must have some degree of competency but explains that being "book smart and street dumb" can also have its pitfalls.

She was always fascinated with muscles. Lynne said, "As a kid I was energetic and strong. I had a natural eagerness to compete, which I did. As a member of the varsity women's basketball team in

Shoulder shrugs work Lynne's trapezius muscles.

Lynne Pirie

college, it became obvious that I needed more upper-body strength. My coach agreed and marched me into the weight room. After showing me a handful of basic barbell exercises, she left me to it, the only female in the gym. I was eighteen years old. There may have been a few chauvinistic smirks during my first workouts, but my seriousness showed through sufficiently to quell any smart remarks. Besides, I was getting stronger. Pretty soon the men in the gym were confiding to me that they wished their girlfriends would train with weights. Acknowledgments like this kept me training harder than ever."

When the spring term ended, Lynne went home for the summer. Immediately, she got a job and then searched out, and miraculously found, a perfect gym in her own small town. It was owned by Jim and Julia Pappas, a husband-and-wife team who were well informed about bodybuilding. Julia took Lynne under her wing and redesigned her program to cover every body part from head to toe. She trained regularly with her best friend at the time.

Back in college, Lynne met a young black woman named Patsy Chapman, who also liked to work out with weights. Although they didn't get along at first, they became workout partners, then good friends. The two women heard about a contest in Canton, Ohio. It was one of the first hardcore bodybuilding contests for women. The promoter, Henry McGhee, said that the women would be judged like men, and they were. Then came George Snyder's Best in the World contest. Lynne didn't place well at all, and was naturally disappointed, but Patsy came in first, and Lynne was happy for her.

After placing seventh in the AAU American National Championships in Atlantic City (which Rachel McLish won),

Lynne performs shoulder presses on a Nautilus machine.

Lynne attained her first victory at the Miss Pittsburgh contest. This was in 1981, the same year that George Snyder had told her she was too tall (5 feet 8 inches) to win anything.

Then Lynne met trainer Jerry Doyle in Phoenix, and she reached a new plateau in her progress. In her best-selling book *Getting Built* (Warner Books, New York), Ms. Pirie credits Doyle's methods with transforming her physique. He is still her coach today.

In 1982, she won third place in the world championships, beating Carla Dunlap. She also won the California Gold Cup and capped off her year of successes by winning the Miss USA title.

Lynne's ideal contest weight is between 140–145 pounds. She weighs up to 155 between contests, but never more. Her favorite foods include fresh and dried fruit, cheese, red meat, oatmeal cookies, and yogurt-covered almonds. She also eats salads and seafood. The only brand of yogurt she'll eat is Yoplait. Occasionally, she will allow herself the dubious luxury of her all-time favorite dessert—cheesecake.

Lynne rarely eats a big meal. She snacks four or five times a day, and supplements her diet with Joe Weider's Musclebuilder protein and high-quality amino acids. She doesn't have the time to cook. Her day has to be organized to accommodate her busy schedule. She's up every morning at 5:30 A.M. to train for 1½ hours at Jerry Doyle's health club in Phoenix.

She has a syndicated newspaper column, *Dr. Lynne Pirie's Fitness Forum*,

When Lynne trains, she trains hard. She rests for 30 seconds or less between exercises. She usually does eight reps per set, but she sometimes tries for a maximum press on the bench for just a single rep. She does straight sets for squats and always does supersets for her arms.

Steve Reeves was Lynne's first inspiration. She also respects Albert Beck-

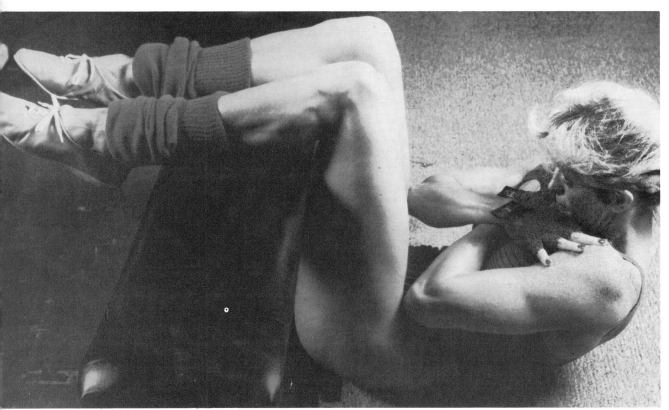

Crunches work Lynne's abdominals.

in dozens of newspapers in the United States. She is a sportscaster for numerous television specials dealing with strength training and bodybuilding. On top of everything, Lynne has a full-time job with her sports medicine practice, which has at times kept her on 36–48-hour shifts or performing surgery. At the end of her work day, she trains again, this time at the gym in her clinic.

les, for his longevity in the sport, and Lou Ferrigno. Most of all, Arnold Schwarzenegger is the one from whom she has learned the most. She said, "I just like Arnold's tenacity. Whatever he undertakes, he does it with a winning attitude. And even in the midst of promoting a show, a film, or a book, he will find time to portray bodybuilding in a positive way."

Lynne poses at an IFBB Ms. Olympia competition.

Lynne Pirie

As a qualified doctor, Lynne Pirie could prescribe for herself virtually *any* type of drug to enhance her training. She's very aware of what bodybuilders take. She does not take synthetic hormones (steroids) of any kind. Why? Because of the androgenic effect. She told us, "They influence the development of the secondary sex characteristics associated with males—a deeper voice, increased facial hair, increased masculinity, susceptibility to male pattern baldness, increased hemoglobin levels in the blood, heavier bones, a more masculine body line, more body hair. And once someone stops taking steroids, often the body's own hormone production has been slowed or shut down, particularly the adrenal glands and the ovaries. Additionally, the possible ill effects on the reproductive system are very real. There may be an effect on unborn children, such as hypermasculinization of the fetus. That can be tragic, especially if it's a female child."

This brings us to what constitutes the ideal woman's physique. Is it the muscular Bev Francis or the more feminine Rachel McLish? Lynne commented, "Actually, I enjoyed seeing Bev in the film *Pumping Iron II—The Women*, but my own taste is for a slightly leaner look. But I do like full muscles. Women like Marjo Selin, Carolyn Cheshire, Gladys Portugues, and Carla Dunlap have great bodies, yet they do not take steroids. I guess that's the bottom line for me. I do not like the drug scene, nor the type of body that drugs create."

Even though her life is as full as it can be, Dr. Lynne Pirie has some goals to achieve. She hopes to do well in the IFBB Ms. Olympia contest. She wants to expand her present medical facility by way of increased television exposure. Lynne agrees that bodybuilding success today is difficult, but she will keep at it because she loves it. The hardest part for her is choreographing her routine—it's so time consuming.

Whenever possible, Lynne promotes bodybuilding: "We women are no longer afraid to be naturally beautiful. In fact, we're training like fighters to be so. Dieting or calisthenics are not good enough if we want to be fully toned. It doesn't work after our teen years because the firmness of youth has gone. Only progressive-resistance training can bring it back. Nothing works as well. Nothing feels as good. That's why my axiom '*Behind every worthwhile curve is a muscle*' is a principle I adhere to every day. Bodybuilding with weights has no substitute!"

Lynne does push-ups on the grass for her triceps.

Lynne Pirie's Diet

Breakfast

Oatmeal (hot)
Raisins and dates
Coffee (½ cup)

Lunch

Salad
Tuna fish
Piece of fruit

Dinner

Broiled chicken
Rice
Green or yellow vegetables
Coffee

Late Evening Snack

Protein drink (occasionally) made with 8 oz. milk, 2 Tbsp. milk-and-egg protein mix with fruit flavoring (bananas, strawberries, peaches, etc.)

Lynne Pirie's Routine

Frequency

Three days of training per week in the off season; six days per week prior to a contest.

Split System

Her routine is split according to her work schedule.

WARM-UP	Sets	Reps
Stationary Bicycle (5 minutes)		
CHEST		
Nautilus Chest Machine	5 ×	8–10
Nautilus Bench Press	4 ×	8–10
SHOULDERS		
Nautilus Double Shoulder Machine	3 ×	10–15
Nautilus Rowing Torso Machine	2 ×	15
Nautilus Overhead Press	3 ×	12–20
BACK		
Nautilus Pullover Machine	4 ×	10
Nautilus Pulldown Machine	4 ×	10
Seated Cable Pulley Row	3 ×	8–12
ARMS		
Nautilus Biceps Curl Machine	6 ×	10–15
Nautilus Multi-purpose Machine (wrist curls, extensions)	3 ×	10–15
THIGHS		
Nautilus Hip/Back Machine	3 ×	10
Nautilus Squat Machine	3 ×	12–15
Leg Curl	3 ×	10–15
Leg Extension	3 ×	15
CALVES		
Standing Calf Raise	6 ×	15–20
Seated Calf Raise	6 ×	15–20
ABDOMINALS		
Seated Broomstick Twist	1 ×	200
Hanging Leg Raise	6 ×	20
Nautilus Abdominal Machine	6 ×	20

An alternate dumbbell forward raise . . .

A seated barbell press . . .

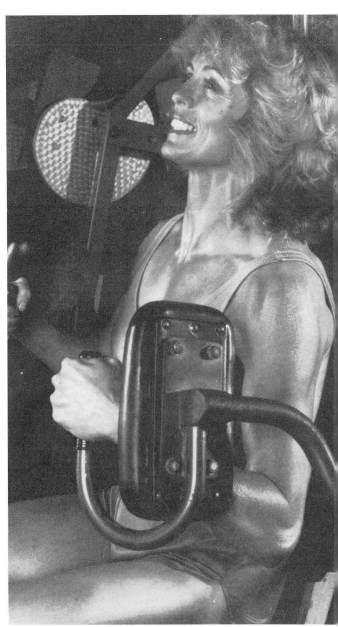

And lateral raises on a Nautilus machine.

TINA PLAKINGER

The Free Spirit

"I don't have time for those prima-donna bodybuilders," said Tina Plakinger. "You know, the women who act like big-shot celebrities . . . I'm down to earth. I'll never forget where I came from. I had it tough as a kid."

Honesty is a very big part of Tina Plakinger's personality. She was born into a world with very little promise on September 29, 1957. Her birthplace was Milwaukee, Wisconsin. She has two sisters, Theresa, age thirty-three, who lives on a farm and keeps fit by chopping wood, and Patty, age twenty-four, who does a little weight training to keep in shape. Tina went to school in Wautoma, a small town with an Indian heritage.

Tina described her initiation into bodybuilding: "Three days before my eighteenth birthday, I got into bodybuilding. As a child I had come to know about weight training because my father had a set of weights at home, and I would help him out now and again if he needed a lift. Then one day a 2½-pound weight fell on my foot and broke my toe. That was it for me.

"With my eighteenth year looming ahead, I got back. I joined a gym because I didn't want to do the singles bar scene. I wanted to meet people . . . but more than that, I was angry with life. I needed to let off steam. I was becoming introverted and disillusioned. I began to feel better about myself. I was a natural. I was raised on a farm, naturally strong and full of energy. Now, at last, I had found something to absorb my frustrations. I love strength training."

Tina shows off with a casual pose.

Tina read every book and magazine she could get her hands on. One book, *Bodybuilding for Women* by Steve Davis, was given to her by a friend. She followed it to the word—it was her bible.

"I went to Vic Tanny's almost every day. I'd bring along my own two-by-four wood plank for squats with me every day. I was a very powerful girl . . . but soon I outgrew the gym. So I went to the Reseda Gold's Gym in California. I need a real hardcore gym. It's the *only* place I can train. I still have the occasional workout at Gold's or World's in Santa Monica. They're great gyms, too," Tina said.

Tina used to work at a health-food store, Nutrition World, so she got her vitamins and supplements at discount prices. At home she would eat every-

What an arm!

Tina works her shoulders with a cable lateral raise.

thing in sight, with a particular penchant for eggs. Her parents watched her new-found hobby, realizing how important it was to her, but the one thing that bothered her father was her constant eating habit.

In her early training days, Tina would run two miles every day, meditate, then train. She developed quickly, but she was eating too much pasta. She realized that she needed more tuna, chicken, and fish, and changed her diet.

When Tina started working at a different health-food store, Wedgewood Nutrition, the owner soon fell in love with her. Three weeks later he proposed and four weeks later they were married.

Tina told us, "My husband ran a show called Ms. Mid America. I won the short class and a comparative newcomer, Cory Kneuer, later to become Cory Everson, won the tall class and the overall title. From then on, I entered a slew of amateur contests, culminating in the AAU Ms. America. I was so thrilled that day. After that, I turned pro. I was bubbling with joy when Ben Weider sent my pro card to me. Here I was, a rough,

tough 5-foot 4-inch punk, with a profession. I was really one of the top bodybuilders in the world. My pride was enormous."

Tina Plakinger came into bodybuilding from nothing. That's how she describes it. Today she is a world champion, with her eyes set on the Ms. Olympia title. She also gets work in commercials, videos, and television via her agent (John Forse, Athletes Registry Inc., Los Angeles, CA). Why is she getting this kind of work when she has no formal training in the acting and show-business field? Because Tina is honest, openminded, and real. She's good at it. Her

Heavy T-bar rows make Tina's back brawny!

latest creation is *Woman of the Future*, an aerobics and weight-training video for Royce American Productions.

One way in which Ms. Plakinger differs from other women bodybuilders is that she believes in bulking up between shows. Her ideal contest weight is 127 pounds. She builds herself to 145 pounds between shows but still looks good—there's no extra fat or flab. The Plakinger physique is still hard and firm and feminine. She gains weight by training very hard and by eating five times a day. She loves Tofutti (frozen tofu), which she eats with sliced banana. As a treat she may occasionally have fettuccine, but actually she's a real protein buff. She takes amino acids and Joe Weider's vegetable protein powder as supplements every day.

"I train every morning at 8:30 for 1½–2 hours, six days a week, with Sundays off. Just before a contest I train twice each day. My reps are usually around ten but these increase to 12–15 as show-time approaches," Tina said. After being beaten by Mary Roberts in the Toronto World Championships in what the magazines termed a controversial decision, Tina's spirits were low. Then she spoke with Franco Columbu one day. He told her that he, too, was down in spirits a couple of times after being defeated in debatable decisions. He told her that she needed a good run in the mountains. Franco gave her some advice about contest preparation, training, and nutrition.

"Apart from my husband, Bob, who has been a wonderful support, I have to thank Frank Zane for being my role model. No one, man or woman, has equalled his streamlined physique. After copying Zane's methodology and some of his posing, I met him at a show . . . and as I came off stage he said: 'Great posing, Tina. I should get some tips from you!' What a turnaround of circumstances!" Tina said.

Arnold Schwarzenegger is another one that she admires. Several years ago she heard him say that he was doing ten sets of heavy calf work for his lower legs. From that day, she did the same . . . and it's working.

It's been eleven years of training so far for Tina. She doesn't do forced reps, but she does push to the max, believing that the mind can push the body to enormous limits, making forced reps unnecessary. Tina does loads of supersets, not on squats, which are done with straight sets, but on most other exercises. She takes very little rest between sets. Few people can keep up with her training.

"Bodybuilding is the toughest sport there is," contended Tina. "There's no off-season like football. Those guys relax half the year and then go off to training camp to get back into it! Bodybuilding's a year-round thing. And on top of heavy training you have to pretty well be an artist and a nutritionist as well. You need a ton of mental discipline, too. There are a lot of good trainers in the gym who will never be champions because they lack the mental discipline to diet."

On the subject of masculinity in women's bodybuilding, Tina likes mass, but with one proviso: well-proportioned muscles should highlight a female figure. The hardest part of her training is getting the energy during those last few weeks when her calorie intake is cut low. But her inner need for success is so positive that she gets through it. "I may not be the most intellectual person in the world, but I'm up there with genuine feeling and gratitude. I'm not self-righteous or puritanical . . . no prima donna . . . well, perhaps at contest time when I'm ripped and ready. . . . Then I may allow myself the luxury of feeling *totally superior*!"

Tina Plakinger's Diet

Breakfast

4-egg omelet (with
   varied ingredients)
6 slices bacon
Hash-browned potatoes
Orange juice

Post-Workout Snack

Protein drink:
   2 cups pineapple juice
   Joe Weider's vegetable protein
     powder
   2 raw eggs
   1 large banana

Lunch

Tuna or chicken salad
   (with diet mayonnaise,
   peas, and pasta)
Whole-wheat pita bread
1 Weider Blaster Pak Bar
Iced tea (artificially
   sweetened)

Dinner

1 large roasted chicken
   (with ketchup)
1 large baked potato
   (with cheese and bacon bits)
½ cantaloupe

Snack

(2 or 3 times per week)
1–2 pints Tofutti (frozen tofu)
   (with sliced bananas)
     or
Dietetic cookies

Tina has fantastic back definition.

Notes

Approximately fifteen weeks prior to a contest, she increases her aerobic exercises and supplements her diet with fat burners and Joe Weider Anabolic Mega-Paks, which help to reduce body fat. About ten weeks before a show, she cuts back on butter, sour cream, salad dressing, and other high-fat foods.

— Tina Plakinger's Routine —

Frequency

Three consecutive days of training, one day of rest.

Split System

Day one: chest and back; day two: shoulders and arms; day three: legs.

Superheavy squats . . . Tina Plakinger style.

Day One

CHEST	Sets	Reps
Incline Press	4	× 10
Incline Flye	4	× 10
Pec-Deck Flye	4	× 10
Cable Crossover	4	× 10

BACK		
Chin	4	× 10
Wide-grip Lat Pulldown	4	× 10
Close-grip Lat Pulldown	4	× 10
T-Bar Row	4	× 10

Day Two

SHOULDERS		
Dumbbell Lateral Raise	4	× 10
Military Press	4	× 10
Bent-over Cable Pull	4	× 10

BICEPS		
Preacher Bench Curl	4	× 10
Alternate Dumbbell Curl	4	× 10
Cable Curl	4	× 10

TRICEPS		
Triceps Extension	4	× 10
French Press (dumbbell)	4	× 10
Close-grip Pushdown	4	× 10

FOREARMS		
Wrist Curl	3	× 10
Reverse Wrist Curl	3	× 10

Day Three

THIGHS		
Lunge	4	× 10
Squat	4	× 10
Leg Extension	4	× 10
Lying Leg Curl	4	× 10
Standing Leg Curl	4	× 10

CALVES		
Standing Calf Raise	5	× 10
Seated Calf Raise	5	× 10

Standing leg curls really work Tina's leg biceps.

Wide-grip lat pulldowns performed by Tina.

GLADYS PORTUGUES

Taking It to the Max

"**I** just sat there, fascinated," said Gladys Portugues. "The 1980 Ms. Olympia contest, the very first one, was on television. I was awestruck!"

The next morning a twenty-three-year-old Gladys joined the nearest gym. It happened to be a Nautilus gym, right in the heart of New York City, her home town.

She was born on the island of Manhattan on September 30, 1957, and until she visited the gym she knew nothing about progressive-resistance exercise. She didn't even know there were such things as free weights, let alone huge machines, particularly for conditioning muscles.

Gladys wanted to be just like the women of the 1980 Ms. Olympia contest. She had grown up among four sisters, Denise, Verna, Sonia, and Ira Sena, plus one brother, Juan. "I was always a happy kid. I loved track and volleyball. I was very fast. In volleyball they used to call me *short stop*," she said.

She went to the New York High School of Art and Design and then on to Marymount Manhattan College. However, her progress was so fast in body-building that she left after a year. Her parents understood. They always knew she would end up getting involved in a physical vocation, and they approved.

Gladys trained hard on the Nautilus machines, but her progress was not as noticeable as she would have liked—she wanted to add mass. Gladys experimented with free weights and found them to do a better job for her than the

Gladys runs in the sand for her calves and legs.

That's a wild pose, Gladys Portugues!

machines. Then she joined the Better Bodies Gym (12 West 21st St., New York, NY), which was run by business entrepreneur Brian Moss.

Gladys said about her early training, "I was real strong from the beginning. Most people start with about twenty pounds, for example, in the shoulder press. But the first time I did it I was using sixty—and I weighed under a hundred pounds."

Her very first contest was the National Gym Association's show in New York. Although she didn't place in the final standings, she was awarded the trophy for the most symmetrical physique. After more hard training, she entered Wayne DeMilia's amateur Night of Champions in New York City and, to her amazement, she won. Onward bound, Gladys placed well in the Caesar's World Cup in Las Vegas, Nevada, and as a result appeared in the movie *Pumping Iron II— The Women*.

The next development in her career occurred when Bob Kennedy recommended that Ken Wheeler, the owner of Canada's largest chain of gyms—Super Fitness, arrange to have Gladys make a television commercial for his gyms. The two got along so well together that Gladys now regards Ken as her trainer. Brian Moss still manages the business aspect and modelling bookings of her career.

Gladys amazed the world by placing seventh at the 1984 Ms. Olympia contest in Montreal. In fact, Wayne DeMilia had lamented the IFBB decision to let her compete at all, stating that she would be totally outclassed. But she was ripped and ready. Her hair was pulled back flat against her head to make her shoulders look even broader. Her posing caused quite a stir.

Actually, Gladys's tumultuous improvement and weight increase had all her critics claiming that she was on steroids. . . . The very idea of steroids is abhorrent to her. If only they knew the torturous training Ken Wheeler had put her through, and that her total increase in weight from her previous show was only one pound!

Food is a subject dear to Gladys's heart. She loves it! Having a real penchant for Italian food, she especially likes veal cutlet parmigiana and spaghetti (with Prego sauce) with bread and butter and Parmesan cheese. Spinach lasagna is another favorite but her abso-

Gladys wins her first big show at Wayne DeMilia's Night of Champions.

Brian Moss helps Gladys with her dumbbell shoulder presses.

lute preference is spaghetti with meat and banana.

Of course, as a contest gets closer everything gets stripped away. Gladys finds fish to be too bland, especially when it is boiled or cooked without butter and sauces. So her precontest diet invariably comes down to one solitary food: chicken breasts (without the skin). Overall, she tries to eat five or six small meals a day. Her training supplements include a multiple-vitamin pill, amino acids, chelated minerals, calcium lactate, iron pills, and vitamin C.

At training time before contests, when she increases to two workouts a day, Gladys likes to perform about ten reps per exercise for the upper body and several more reps when working her legs. The only time she does forced reps is prior to competition. For the most part, she prefers straight sets rather than supersets or pre-exhaust training.

She told us, "Brian Moss has been the vital force in my career, but I put my body entirely in Ken Wheeler's hands when I want to compete. He knows everything about training. Vince Gironda is another guy who makes good sense to me. Bob Kennedy, too, has the odd piece of good advice!"

Ms. Portugues has her own book, co-authored with Joyce Vedral, a trade paperback entitled *Hard Bodies* (Dell Publishing Co., New York). It's must reading for every woman who wants to start training with weights. Gladys has appeared in dozens of magazines, including *MuscleMag International, Flex,*

Muscle & Fitness, Vogue, Self, Cosmopolitan, Ms., American Photographer, and *Sport Style*, and she still likes to work in the various media. She yearns to do more commercial work, acting, and television appearances, but beneath it all she's as dedicated as any other competitive bodybuilder. She wants to win the Ms. Olympia contest.

She said, "I think female bodybuilders should be muscular and symmetrical. The overall appearance must not be too ugly. A woman athlete has to have a clean, neat appearance. She must look feminine with muscles in the right places—not drug induced. Even in men I prefer the Bob Paris physique to the blown-out-of-proportion monsters. People like Arnold Schwarzenegger and

Is this how Gladys does her curls?

Rear leg raises work Gladys's glute muscles.

John Terilli look great . . . but some are too much. Reeves had the right idea. What a physique!"

Gladys readily admits that the toughest part of bodybuilding is the strict diet. She finds it hard to get a good pump in her muscles when she has to cut down on carbohydrates. Her energy is lessened. She also confesses to loving bodybuilding more than anything else, and she really enjoys performing.

What is Gladys's final wish for bodybuilding? She said, "I would like to see couples competitions in the Olympics . . . It's beautiful."

Gladys shows excellent form in a triceps pressdown.

Gladys Portugues's Diet

Breakfast

3 eggs (scrambled or boiled)
2 slices whole-wheat bread
  (with butter)
Cappuccino
¼ melon

Lunch

2 chicken breasts
Spaghetti
  (with Prego sauce)
Banana

Dinner

8 oz. (240 g) steak (beef)
Sweet potato
Broccoli

Gladys Portugues

Gladys Portugues's Routine

Frequency

Four days per week.

Split System

Mondays and Thursdays: chest, triceps, legs, and abdominals; *Tuesdays and Fridays*: back, shoulders, biceps, and abdominals.

Monday & Thursday

CHEST	Sets	Reps	Pounds	THIGHS	Sets	Reps	Pounds
Bench Press	1	× 10	× 95	Squat	1	× 10	× 135
	1	× 4	× 105		1	× 8	× 145
	1	× 6	× 115		1	× 6	× 155
	1	× 1–3	× 130		1	× 4	× 175
Incline	1	× 10	× 30	Thigh Extension	1	× 15	× 20
Dumbbell	1	× 8	× 35		1	× 10	× 30
Press	1	× 6	× 40		1	× 8	× 40
	1	× 1–3	× 40		1	× 6	× 50
Flat Bench Flye	2	× 10	× 30		1	× 4–6	× 60
	1	× 8	× 35	Leg Curl	1	× 10	× 10
	1	× 6	× 35		1	× 8	× 15
					1	× 6	× 20
TRICEPS				CALVES			
Close-grip	1	× 15	× 50	Standing Calf	1	× burn	× 200
Pushdown	1	× 10	× 60	Raise	1	× burn	× 260
	1	× 8	× 70		1	× burn	× 300
	1	× 4–6	× 80		1	× burn	× 360
Dumbbell	4	× 6	× 40	Seated Calf Raise	1	× 20	× 100
Extension					1	× 20	× 120
Parallel Bar Dip	4	× 6	× 25		1	× 10	× 150
(with weight)							

ABDOMINALS	Sets	Reps
Twist	4	× 100
Side Bend	4	× 100
Crunch	4	× burn
Leg Raise	4	× burn

Gladys does prone hyperextensions for her lower back.

Tuesday & Friday

BACK	Sets	Reps	Pounds
Chin (with weight)	4	× 4	× 25
Barbell Row	1	× 10	× 95
	3	× 8	× 105
Deadlift	1	× 10	× 135
	1	× 8	× 185
	1	× 4–6	× 225
	1	× 2–4	× 235
	1	× 1–2	× 250

SHOULDERS			
Dumbbell Press	1	× 10	× 30
	1	× 6–8	× 35
	1	× 2–6	× 40
Seated Lateral Raise	2	× 15	× 135
	2	× 20	× 145

BICEPS			
Barbell Curl	1	× 10	× 50
	1	× 8	× 60
	1	× 6	× 70
	1	× 4	× 80
Preacher Bench Curl	3	× 10	× 40

ABDOMINALS
(same as Monday)

MARY ROBERTS

Single-Minded Spirit

Mary does a classic pose.

When Mary Roberts was eleven years old, she and the rest of her family were anxiously awaiting the arrival of a new television set. The man who carried it into their living room had bulging muscles. Almost twenty years later she realized that the guy must have been a bodybuilder. The image of his bulging biceps stayed with her all those years.

Petite Ms. Roberts was born on March 17, 1950, in New Orleans, Louisiana, to a family of three brothers and two sisters. As a youngster, Mary was always physically active. She ran, played baseball, and took part in other sports. Soon the family moved to California where she first attended Artesia High School in Cerritos, then college in the same town. Mary got married, worked at a variety of secretarial jobs, and began bringing up three children—Tina, Ricky, and Cherié René.

After getting married, Mary discovered that she wanted to participate in a demanding physical activity. She joined a health club and got into "jazzercise," an aerobics class. She also worked with exercise machines occasionally, but no free weights were used. At that time, she and her husband were involved in a bicycle import-export business of top-quality bikes and accessories. It seemed quite natural for Mary to take up cycling. She would take her bike for long-distance rides every weekend.

Mary felt so good from her physical exercise that she decided to increase the degree of her training. She tried lifting weights. She explained, "It was like magic. My previous exercise had built

Mary prepares for some squats.

some muscle tone, but now I was developing. Free weights were taking my body somewhere very different. My father, who had been a merchant seaman, a very tough and fit person, to my delight and amusement, said I was *awesome*. He encouraged my family to take part in sports of all kinds. My mother, a conservative Catholic of French and Indian descent, was not quite so keen on my new-found hobby. But she's turned around now, although I still suspect she's not completely happy about my appearing on stage with so little clothing."

When Mary first started bodybuilding with weights, she did her best to learn everything she could about the sport. She read books and magazines. Her brothers did some training and she learned from them. She did the basic exercises (bench presses, squats, Military presses, etc.) when she went to the gym, but it didn't take long for her to realize that she knew more than the instructors. She no longer felt at ease taking their advice. She went her own way. As a result she lost inches, but looked tighter and firmer. Her arms got bigger and her back widened.

It was ironic how Mary began entering contests. Californian promoter Mike Glass was running a European-style contest. Serge Nubret's wife, Jacqueline, had won it the previous year. She was considered to have an ideal physique by the judges. She is a classically beautiful woman with nice lines, femininity, and muscle tone. Mary was training hard to enter this contest. She described what transpired:

"I hit the weights so hard that my body just *took off*. Muscles were popping out all over. Within a month I realized that I had outpaced the judges' standards of idealism. In reality, I was a little bit more rounded and toned than Jacqueline Nubret *before* I had even lifted a weight. But now I was way more built . . . and ripped, too. Realizing how ahead of my time I was, I didn't enter the contest."

Actually, Mary's first contest was the second Robby Robinson Classic in 1980. She finished second to Kay Baxter. Then, in 1981, she entered and won the Ms. Western America, and a few week later swept to victory in the AAU Ms. America show, winning the lightweight class. Carla Dunlap won the heavyweight class and the overall title.

According to the *Female Physique Athlete* (by Al Thomas and Steve Wennerstrom): "Mary Roberts will be looked up in the future as a woman who was well ahead of her time in the women's bodybuilding world."

The 1985 World Women's Championships held in Toronto, Canada, saw Mary reach the pinnacle of success. She became world champ, beating a very conditioned Tina Plakinger and two "new breed" bodybuilders, Vera Bendal of Germany and Deanna Panting of Canada.

Her ideal body weight is around 121 pounds and she's 5 feet 3 inches tall. Being in the beauty business (Mary teaches cosmetology and exercise), she has access to specific apparatus to measure her body-fat content). Measuring body fat with calipers at various sites is helpful in knowing superfluous fat content under the skin, but it doesn't tell you about the fat content in the muscle. She finds hydrostatic (water submersion) measurements to be the most accurate.

Mary seldom takes her weight higher than 15 pounds above her contest weight. When she does exhibitions, she

Her rear deltoids are worked with bent-over raises.

will be a very toned 130 pounds. Right now she is not striving to be bigger. Coming down to her contest weight is not difficult because she has a fast metabolism.

Mary told us about her eating habits: "I like chicken, sometimes fish. I did

The hack machine effectively exercises Mary's legs.

eat fish and baked potatoes prior to winning the 1985 World Women's Championships. I eat beef rarely in the off-season, and I'm not too keen on milk by-products. I like to eat every 2½–3 hours to keep my energy level high. Only very occasionally will I eat ice cream, candy, or cookies. I'll do it and forget it. There is no guilt trip. Moderation is the key."

One thing Mary does believe in is vitamins. She takes a daily multi-pack of supplements and in addition takes vitamins C, B, calcium, zinc, and magnesium. She takes tryptophan every night (the amino acid that helps to induce sleep popularized by bodybuilder Frank Zane) and octosonal for endurance. When dieting for a show, she will take large doses of vitamin B_{15}.

She said, "Most of my protein is taken via regular meals and snacks, but occasionally I will mix a protein powder with yogurt for an additional supply. I take amino acids all year round." Mary talks quite a lot about her supplementation in her seminars.

Mary once had a lower-back problem that required surgery, so she is very careful to warm up before her workouts. She stretches every morning and usually does her workout at that time, too. Like virtually every other top woman bodybuilder, she trains three days on, one day off. But she listens to her body. If she needs it, she will take two days off. Her reps are varied deliberately. The usual format involves her training with six reps until she can increase it to eight. Then more weight is added so that she can again only manage six.

Currently, Mary is not training her upper body with heavy weights. But she is training her legs vigorously. In the off season she does low reps for squats, two or three warm-up sets of ten reps, then uses maximum weight for six reps. Early in her career she had fatty hamstring muscles in her legs, but with hard training and good nutrition she has conquered the problem.

On the subject of forced reps, this world champion is adamant: I do *not* use forced reps anymore. I used to, but I found that they brought on injuries. Tendons and ligaments are like rubber bands. They take so much . . . then break. I see people in the gym swinging the barbells up and down. They could have a thousand pounds on the bar but it's not doing them any good. You can't beat a good solid full-range-of-motion exercise style. It works the belly of the muscle and brings results."

We wanted to know about Mary's contest preparation. Obviously she has found the secret. She explained, "Basically, I gradually lower my calorie content for all foods. Then I cut out the high-calorie foods altogether. I have a fast metabolic rate and my weight comes down easily. But if by chance it's not coming down the way I want, I will train my *whole* body each day for the last five days, but using light weights. This drops the water. I train light because energy is low and because dehydrated muscles can suffer small injuries if trained heavy. I also get preventative maintenance in the form of chiropractic adjustments—ultrasound, body massage, and facial massage."

Mary Roberts is, by her own admission, a perfectionist. She learns from everyone, but one person recently has played a special part in her career—Tom Nista. "He's wonderful. I've never had a male friend to support me in my bodybuilding efforts. Tom is behind me 100 percent. He's a great friend."

Women's bodybuilding is at a crossroad; the direction is uncertain. Regardless of where one may want it to go, other influences can change its course. Mary sees all the name bodybuilders as

Look at Mary's incredible back as she does a standing leg curl.

great: "They have their different structures—some more pleasing than others. Muscularity is just a small part of it. It's the whole package and how it's presented that counts with the judges."

Mary once did a lot of personalized training with her clients at one time, but found that she was becoming frustrated because many were not good listeners.

Mary Roberts

She said, "They had so many personal problems that it drained me. So now I'm more into the beauty field. I design clothing, do beauty shows and photo-modelling work, things nothing to do with bodybuilding."

No one would dispute that Mary Roberts has high morals. She would never sell out. She has an inborn respect for herself, a high self-esteem. She gives her all to be the very best she can. Nothing can stop or sway her. She likes to be happy and see people that way. Life is too short to be otherwise. Her own conclusion to the sport of women's bodybuilding? "I just want to perform, to do my best. I like to win. I just do it!"

Mary Roberts can be contacted about seminars or questions at: P.O. Box 10493, Santa Ana, CA 92711.

Mary Roberts's Diet

Breakfast

½ cup oatmeal
1 medium banana
1 cup orange juice

Mid-Morning Snack

½ cup of non-fat yogurt
¼ cup fresh fruit
6 oz. (180 g) chicken

Lunch

6 oz. (180 g) turkey
Green salad
½ cup brown rice

Mid-Afternoon Snack

Protein shake
  (made with egg protein)

Dinner

8 oz. (240 g) fish or chicken
1 baked potato (plain)
½ cup cooked green vegetables

Supplements

4 amino acid tablets
  (after every meal except
  her mid-afternoon snack)
Super multi-pack vitamins
  (at breakfast and dinner)

—Mary Roberts's Routine—

Frequency
Three days of training, one day of rest.

Split System
Mary splits her routine into three parts, performing one part per workout.

Workout Routine

CHEST	Sets Reps		BICEPS	Sets Reps
Incline Smith Press	4 × 8–10		Incline Dumbbell Curl	3 × 10
Flat Dumbbell Press	3 × 8		Standing Barbell Curl	3 × 10
Dumbbell Flye on Pec-Deck	3 × 10		Nautilus Compound Curl	3 × 10
Dumbbell Pullover	3 × 10			
			THIGHS	
SHOULDERS			Leg Extension	3 × 12–15
Standing Rear Cable Lateral	3 × 12		Leg Press	4 × 15–20
			Squat	4–5 × 8
Standing Dumbbell Side Lateral	3 × 10–12		Standing Leg Curl	4 × 10
			Lying Leg Curl	3–4 × 12
Bent-over Dumbbell Lateral	3 × 10		Dumbbell Lunge	3 × 10
Seated Military Press behind Neck	3 × 10–12			
			CALVES	
			Seated Calf Raise	5 × 12–15
BACK			Standing Calf Raise	4 × 12–15
Close-grip Pulldown	3–4 × 12		Donkey Calf Raise	4 × 10–12
Pulldown behind Neck	3 × 10			
Bent-over Barbell Row	4 × 10		ABDOMINALS	
One-arm Dumbbell Row	3 × 12		Cable Crunch	4 × 25
			Decline Sit-up	4 × 20
			Knee Raise	4 × 25
TRICEPS				
Triceps Pushdown	3–4 × 12			
Lying Dumbbell French Press	3 × 10			
Cable Kickback	3 × 10–12			

MARJO SELIN

The Queen of Iron

She hails from northern Europe—tall and possibly one of the most beautiful of all the professional women bodybuilders. Her appearance is strong yet elegant—she is unmistakably feminine.

Marjo Selin was born on October 2, 1960, in Eura, Finland, a small country village near the coastal town of Bori. She grew up among a very sports-minded family, including younger brother Hannu, sister Minna, and half brother Vesa. The whole family played volleyball and went cross-country skiing in the winter months.

Marjo told us how she started bodybuilding. "After graduating from senior high school in 1979 and entering college, something happened that was to change my life. I injured my back, and although it wasn't serious, I was in quite a lot of pain. The medical staff at college put me on a conditioning program using light weights and special movements for the lower back area. I thoroughly enjoyed the vigorous exercise and after a couple of months my boyfriend at the time, Hannu, noticed that I was getting muscles. He had already been training with weights for several years, and seeing the new shape of my body, we decided that I should train on an all-around bodybuilding program. Hannu wrote me out a routine. After six months I had literally transformed my body. My mother was worried that what I was doing was unnatural . . . that I might hurt myself."

Then came Finland's first-ever women's bodybuilding competition—the Helsinki Gym Cup. All the news media were there. First place went to Kiki

Any pose that Marjo does is a memorable picture.

Elomaa, and to Marjo's amazement she came in second. Suddenly, Marjo had become very preoccupied with body-building, and to make her new-found hobby even sweeter, her mother, Raija, began to accept her as a bodybuilder. Now she was proud of Marjo's accomplishments.

From those early college days when she was limited to a leg press machine, a single barbell set, two dumbbells, a flat bench, and a hyperextension unit, Marjo's training took on a more serious note. She trained hard and consistently, taking advice from her boyfriend, Hannu, and from one of Finland's top bodybuilders, Jorma Räty. She said, "He's been a great influence in my training, and so, of course, has Kiki Elomaa. Kiki is a very famous woman in Finland. She's been on the cover of every magazine. She's a household word to the Finnish people. It was Kiki who was responsible for the popularity of women's bodybuilding in my country."

Marjo Selin, like any serious woman bodybuilder, is seeking one day to win the coveted Ms. Olympia title. Although she is proud of her win at the 1981 Finnish Championships, the same year she married Hannu, she wants to take body-building further. She said, "I want to make it my livelihood—to be more and more involved in it. Of course, the Olympia is important, but whether I win it or not depends on which direction the sport goes. I have not taken and will not take anabolic steroids or any growth-promoting drugs. How can I take a drug that could kill me, or damage my liver irreversibly? Besides, one day I want to have children and I would not jeopardize their health for anything—let alone a trophy and a fleeting glimpse of fame as a Ms. Olympia."

Marjo Selin checks the body-building magazines to glean the latest news and information. She also talks to professionals and amateurs alike to gather knowledge from all sources. Then she uses what she considers worthwhile and discards what isn't.

When confronted with the question of femininity and women's body-building, Marjo admitted that it's all very confusing: "I like muscles and I like femininity. I have to admit that I am a little taken back when I see a woman who is rock hard and obviously loaded with testosterone, but, on the other hand, I do enjoy seeing muscles on a woman. Corinna Everson comes to mind when I think of the outer limits of our sport. I think she has the ultimate in both femininity and musculature. She looks great!"

Marjo is an advocate of men's body-building, too. She thinks the sport is ideal for any health-minded young man. Again, though, she has reservations about overdevelopment. She commented, "I prefer the male physique that has been built symmetrically. I don't like huge pecs or thighs unless all the other muscles are developed in proportion. There are many bodybuilders who just go crazy with a mixture of basic power moves and steroids . . . and achieve an almost deformed look. All bodybuilders should work the entire body. Too many of them neglect forearms, calves, hamstrings, abdominals . . . and some even neglect their shoulders, one of the most important areas for masculine impressiveness."

Marjo Selin's workout starts at 5:30 in the afternoon. Two hours later she is in the shower. She trains three days in a row and then rests for one. Because of her previous back injury, she is very aware of the importance of warming up. The first two sets of every exercise are really preparatory introduction to the heavier succeeding sets. Because she wants to add more size and thickness to her muscles, Marjo has a preference for low reps—often as low as six to eight. She does, however, admit to the value of higher reps as an additional boost, and will often use higher repetitions on supplementary exercises such as crossover pulleys or laterals, or at any time when she feels a particular body part could

Marjo relaxes before a workout.

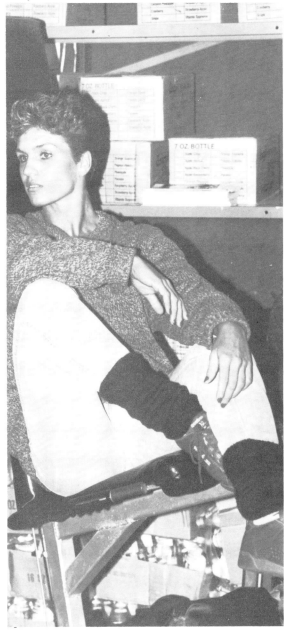

Squats are a must for leg development.

benefit from it. Calves and abdominals are always worked with higher reps.

Between contests, Marjo likes to be about ten pounds over her competition weight. She usually enters at around 138 pounds and has aspirational visions of competing at a little over 140—ripped. Although she is aware of the vast array of principles used in training, Marjo still prefers to train using straight sets in most workouts. She only uses supersets for abdominals and calves, otherwise she just likes to do several sets of the same exercise until she has exhausted the muscle.

As for food, this Finnish national champion eats well, to say the least. Her favorite bodybuilding foods are the staples—steak and potatoes. "But," she said almost apologetically, "I do love ice cream. It may not be the ideal bodybuilding food, but sometimes as a little reward for all my hard work, especially after contest time, I will eat quite a lot of it!"

When it comes to training, the most difficult aspect for Marjo is learning to be selfish during the last month before a contest. She confessed, "I have always been a dedicated bodybuilder, but when the Olympia comes up I must learn to be totally self-centered. Competition today is so keen that I must turn off to other people during that last month. Hannu understands and supports me in this, but sometimes I feel like I'm being too harsh when I refuse to talk to gym members between sets or when I fail to find the time to work on diet and training programs for others. It's a matter of priorities."

Another difficulty for Marjo is projecting herself confidently on stage. "I really admire people like Tina Plakinger who can turn on a show for the audience, or Rachel McLish who can manipulate other contestants on stage. Europeans have a tendency to stand back, hoping to be noticed for what they are, but more and more I am realizing that this is not enough. One has to be great physically *and* forceful, too. No one is so good that she can come on stage and sock the judges between the eyes with a few simple poses. You have to be a presence from the minute you walk on stage. When posing, you have to pan the judges with each display. You need eye contact with the audience to relate to them as people. I am, however, improving my stage projection and it appears to be working."

Because props are sometimes used by professional bodybuilders when they go through their routines on stage, much of the news media have difficulty accepting bodybuilding as a sport. This is why the IFBB now has a ruling that props, such as hats, gloves, cloaks, and even animals, are forbidden in national and international competition.

"It makes for a carnival atmosphere," said Marjo. "Bodybuilding is a sport to be taken seriously. It is one of the most gruelling of all, and I agree with the IFBB ruling. If the media are to accept us as a legitimate sport, then the show-business angle should be dropped. Guest posers can use props . . . but not while competing for a title."

Currently, business administration coupled with fashion merchandising is at the head of Marjo's list of priorities besides bodybuilding. She wants to get her college degree in two years. Then her plan is to use her body, fame, and brain in the business world, but whether or not her line will be directly related to bodybuilding is not known yet. Since she enjoys pushing herself to the limits in her workouts, thrills at strenuous exercise, and relishes the discipline of hardcore training, there is little doubt that the same enthusiasm put into her vocational efforts will pay off handsomely.

For those interested in hiring Marjo Selin for seminars or guest appearances, write her at: Box 9560, Friendship Station, Washington, DC 20016.

Marjo Selin's Diet

Breakfast

4 eggs
2 slices of brown bread
1 banana
Coffee

Mid-Morning Snack

6 oz. (180 g) low-fat yogurt
1 apple

Lunch

Broiled chicken or steak
Potatoes or rice
1 slice brown bread
8 oz. (240 ml) skim milk

Mid-Afternoon Snack

Low-fat cottage cheese
   or yogurt
1 apple
Coffee

Late-Afternoon Snack

1 banana or apple
Amino acids, supplements,
   or protein drink

Dinner

Steak or broiled chicken
Potatoes

Supplements

Multi-vitamin/minerals
Vitamin A   Iron
Vitamin B$_6$ Lecithin
Vitamin C   Magnesium
Vitamin D   Pantothenic acid
Vitamin E   Choline
Calcium   Inositol

Marjo Selin

Notes

Six weeks before a contest, Marjo takes choline, inositol, and other amino acids daily. She also takes potassium and drinks distilled water for the last few days prior to competing.

Marjo Selin's Routine

Frequency

Three consecutive days of training, one day of rest.

Split System

Day one: abdominals, chest, shoulders, and triceps; day two: legs; day three: abdominals, biceps, back, and calves.

Marjo Selin

Day One

	Sets Reps
ABDOMINALS	
Crunch	3 × 20
Sit-up	3 × 15–20
Leg Raise (incline)	3 × 15
CHEST	
Bench Press	3 × 10–12
or	3 × 4–6
Incline Bench Press	1 × 10–15
Cable Crossover	3 × 10–15
or	
Pec-Deck Flye	3 × 10–15
Dumbbell Pullover	3 × 10–15
SHOULDERS	
Seated Press behind Neck	2 × 15–20
	3 × 8–10
	1 × 15
Upright Row	1 × 15
(barbell or cable)	3 × 10–12
	1 × 15
Lateral Raise	3 × 10–15
TRICEPS	
Close-grip Bench Press	2 × 15–20
or	
Seated Dumbbell Triceps Stretch	3 × 6–8
Triceps Stretch (between two benches)	3 × 10–15
Triceps Pressdown (supersetting with Barbell or Cable Curl)	3 × 12–15

Day Two

THIGHS	Sets Reps
Squat	3 × 15–20
or	3 × 6–8
Hack Machine	2 × 10–15
Leg Press (machine)	3 × 15–20
Leg Extension	3 × 10
Leg Curl	1 × 15
	3 × 10–12

(She does leg extensions in off-season as a warm-up before squats or hack squats—3 sets × 15–20 reps.)

CALVES	
Standing Calf Raise	3 × 15–20
Seated Calf Raise	3 × 15–20
Donkey Calf Raise	4 × 20–25
Toe Press	3 × 15–20

Day Three

ABDOMINALS	Sets Reps
Roman Chair Sit-up	3 × 20
Cable Crunch	3 × 15–20
Hanging Knee Raise	3 × 20

CALVES	Sets Reps
Seated Calf Raise	4 × 15–20
Donkey Calf Raise	3 × 20

BICEPS	
Barbell Curl	2 × 12–15
	3 × 8–10
	1 × 15
Seated Dumbbell Curl	1 × 15
or	
Preacher Bench Curl	3 × 10
Cable Curl	3 × 15–20
Triceps Pressdown	3 × 15–20

BACK	
Partial Deadlift	3 × 15–20
	3 × 10
Lat Pulldown	2 × 15
	3 × 8–10
	2 × 15
Seated Cable Row	3 × 10–12
Hyperextension	3 × 15–20

(Alternate with Lat Pulldown or Wide-grip Chin-up behind Neck—4–5 sets × 8–10 reps)

Marjo especially enjoys doing barbell curls.

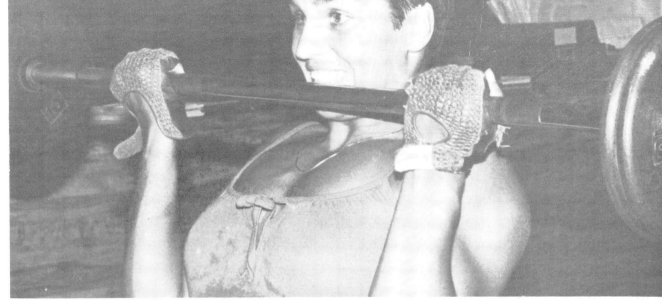

INGER ZETTERQVIST

Symmetry and Size

Swimming was her first love. In fact, from the age of twelve to sixteen, Inger Zetterqvist was a member of the Swedish junior swim team. She enjoyed the stress and strain of competition, excelling at the breast stroke.

Inger was born on February 8, 1957, in Gothenburg, Sweden. She has one sister, Gaby, and grew up in a sports-oriented family, enjoying winter sports as well as summer activities. Her father is a former equestrian champion who had Inger riding almost before she could walk. She still loves being around her father's horses.

When Inger was twenty-three years old she had a leg injury, which she blamed on a skiing accident. It turned out to be a slipped patella. She had an operation to correct the problem. She said, "I had a cast on my leg from my hips to my ankle. When it finally came off, I could hardly recognize my leg. It had shrunk to nothing. My doctor told me that normal life would be fine, but that I would have to guard against aggravating the injury with sports."

Inger didn't enjoy being less than 100 percent fit. She made a special trip to see her doctor, to ask him to give her some exercises to strengthen her knee. However, he sent her home on the bus and wouldn't recommend any exercises for her to do.

In 1980, Inger Zetterqvist couldn't stand her inactivity any more. She went to the Olympia Gym in Gothenburg where two friends helped her devise a simple routine for her leg. She only trained her legs at first, but after a few

Inger sure looks fine surrounded by sun and surf.

Note Inger's outstanding calf development.

weeks she did her whole body, using the basic exercises.

Subsequently, a friend talked her into entering a contest. She had only been training nine months, but she dieted for four months and surprised herself by getting in super form. Inger actually won the contest. That qualified her for the 1981 Swedish Championships, in which she placed fourth. The following year she again took fourth in the same contest, but in 1983 Inger won the European Championships in Malmo, Sweden, then won the Swedish competition. From there, she went on to the World Championships in London and won again. That year she placed third in the Ms. Olympia contest, in which Candy Csenscits was second and Carla Dunlap was first.

Inger stands 5 feet 8 inches tall. When ripped for a contest, she usually weighs about 132 pounds. Between shows, this goes up by 20 pounds or more. She likes being big and strong, and feels better when she is that way. Actually, Inger is always on a partial diet, but when it comes to losing weight for a show she really suffers. She has to diet strictly (1100–1200 calories per day only) for fifteen weeks.

Like many trainers, Inger is a firm advocate of straight sets, using them most of the time. She only uses forced reps when she feels the need to break through a training plateau. Her workout frequency is two days of training, followed by one day of rest. Before a contest, this becomes three days on, one day off. She trains as hard as any man, except that she probably works out with greater enthusiasm and drive prior to a competition.

She uses relatively heavy weights in her training. For example, she can bench press 165 pounds for ten reps, and although this isn't her strongest lift (because of her long arms), it stands as a good example of her overall power.

Like most successful bodybuilders, Inger finds that much of her time is spent keeping her mental attitude on target. She said, "I train with very strict form to isolate each muscle group, and I concentrate deeply throughout each and every set. To train without perfect concentration is a waste of energy, so if my thinking is not 100 percent positive, I leave the gym and come back when I'm able to give everything to my workout, physically and mentally."

She is an avid supporter of men's bodybuilding and is married to Swedish heavyweight champion Matt Kardell. Her priority in life at this time is to raise a healthy family, continue to work in the field of bodybuilding, and to always train hard for top condition.

Have you noticed Inger's incredible abdominals and calf development? Well, truth to tell, she trains neither. She possesses this superiority through natural genetics. Only when a contest is on the horizon will she perform some freestanding calf raises (with no weight) and some abdominal work. This is not to build the areas but to sharpen them.

Bill Reynolds, writer and bodybuilding expert, has high praise indeed for Ms. Zetterqvist: "She's a modern viking," he said. "Marvelously proportioned, physically superior, highly intelligent, sublimely feminine."

Inger Zetterqvist

Inger Zetterqvist's Diet

Off-Season Diet

Breakfast

Oatmeal with fruit
4 slices whole-wheat bread
Protein drink with banana, 2 Tbsp. protein powder, 1 egg, and water

Lunch

4-egg omelet with cheese
Rice

Mid-Afternoon Snack

Cottage cheese
Fruit

Dinner

Chicken or fish
Potatoes, rice, or pasta
Vegetables

Late Evening Snack

Protein drink

Precontest Diet

Breakfast

Oatmeal with fruit
10:00 A.M.: workout (part 1)
1:00 P.M.: nap

Lunch

7 oz. (21 g) fish
3 oz. (90 g) rice (before cooking)
Vegetables

Mid-Afternoon Snack

Fruit
5:00 P.M.: workout (part 2)

Dinner

7 oz. (21 g) fish or chicken
Vegetables

Late Evening Snack

Bread or fruit (amount depends on competition date)

Inger performs crossover-pulley exercises.

—Inger Zetterqvist's Routine—

Frequency

Two days of training followed by one day of rest.

Day One

LEGS	Sets Reps
Squat	3 × 8
Thigh Extension	3 × 8
Thigh Curl	3 × 8

SHOULDERS	
Dumbbell Press	3 × 6
Lateral Raise	2 × 8
Bent-over Lateral	2 × 8

Day Two

BACK	
Lat Machine Pulldown	3 × 6
T-Bar Row	2 × 6
Seated Row	3 × 8

BICEPS	
Barbell Curl	3 × 6
Dumbbell Curl	3 × 6
Concentration Curl	2 × 8

Day Four

CHEST	
Bench Press	3 × 6–8
Incline Dumbbell Press	3 × 6
Dumbbell Flye (lying down)	2 × 8

TRICEPS	
Dumbbell Triceps Extension	2 × 8
Lying Triceps Extension	3 × 6
Triceps Pressdown	2 × 8

Day Five

(same as Day One)

Split System

Two body parts per day, three exercises per body part. Day one: legs, shoulders; day two: back, biceps; day three: rest; day four: chest, triceps; day five: legs, shoulders; day six: rest. When she uses forced reps, she does one exercise per body part.

Flyes on the Pec-Deck machine develop Inger's pectorals.

BECOMING THE BEST

Diana Dennis and Kevin Lawrence

Lynne Pirie

Erika Mes

To succeed in the competitive sport of bodybuilding, you have to "put it all together" to come out on top. You will not win trophies as a result of merely lifting weights, watching for results, and finally strolling on stage at a contest to be handed the first-place prize.

If you have already decided that you want to be a contest-winning bodybuilder, then here's our best advice: *Immerse yourself in the sport*. No matter how convenient it may seem, you cannot secretly train in your basement and then one day suddenly emerge out of the blue to win the Ms. Olympia contest. To be Ms. Olympia, you have to be involved in the sport. You have to know what the latest trends are, diets, and training and posing routines.

By the very fact that you are reading this book, you have already demonstrated a high interest in self-improvement. If you are an upcoming bodybuilder with ambition to compete one day, then take in as many shows as you can. Go to the city and state shows in your area; and don't just attend as a casual observer to be entertained. When you attend a contest as an observer, do just that—*observe*! Make the whole event a learning experience. Check out every competitor. Note how some make themselves stand out from the others, by movement, stance, and charisma. See how those with even-toned dark tans look better than the untanned bodies. Does a particular woman attract the judges' attention more by flexing her muscles? Does she have good posture or a confident smile?

Consider who has chosen the most suitable music to pose to. Often a sensational physique will lose to an inferior one because of a poor presentation. Remember, it is not just the poses you do, but the way that you do them that impresses the judges. A free-posing routine is a combination of ingredients. You have to interpret the music succinctly and learn how to flaunt yourself. There should be a change of pace and element of surprise in your posing routine. You must show grace and vitality. Muscle size and definement must be displayed sufficiently to assure the judges that what they saw in the compulsory pose rounds is still there.

The top bodybuilding stars frequently go to contests of all levels. They seldom go for the entertainment value; their attendance is mainly to learn. Pillow is one woman who travels from one part of the country to another just to see what's happening in the field. Sue Ann McKean does this, too. Corinna Everson is yet another who will do everything reasonable to keep in touch with the sport. You must keep on top of things. Be informed and aware. Ask questions, read books and magazines, look at videos, and attend the IFBB Ms. Olympia contest every year. Sure it's expensive to travel to the contest, but no ambitious bodybuilder has ever regretted his or her decision to attend.

The same goes for your training. Travel occasionally to World's and Gold's gyms in Venice, California. Rub shoulders with the greats. When you train at a commercial gym in your area, make sure that it is the gym where all the action is. Train with a bodybuilder who has contest experience. We are not saying that home training is no good. Many successful bodybuilders have spent years in home training. Gladys Portugues and Candy Csenscits often train extensively at home gyms. It can be very beneficial, especially if you are strongly self-motivated. But as you climb the ladder, then at least most of your precontest training should be done in a well-equipped commercial gym. The atmosphere can help enormously, not to mention the large variety of machines and apparatus.

Join your local chapter of the National Physique Committee. If you feel you are ready to enter contests, then do so. Check your eligibility by reading the entry blanks for the competitions. You can get these by writing to the show promoters who advertise in *Flex* magazine and *MuscleMag International*.

It's far better to compete in small contests at the beginning. Why compete at a level far over your head, where you have a minimal chance of placing? Compete at a local level until you win, then move up. But don't fall into the trap of competing every couple of weeks. Many trophy-hungry women fall into the trap of competing too frequently. Pick your contests carefully and allow room for improvement between shows.

Precontest Preparation Tips

Bill Reynolds, editor of *Muscle & Fitness* magazine, said: "Peaking perfectly for a competition is an art form. It takes several attempts at peaking for competition to get it exactly right. No one reaches an optimum peak on her first attempt."

The general rule is to learn from each peaking experience. There are so many factors that may influence the result. And since you are a unique person with your own metabolism and mental determination, you will have to tailor our advice to your own needs.

Calorie Cutting

Decrease your overall amount of food intake gradually about two or three months prior to a show. Never suddenly drop from 3000 calories daily to 1000. It's far better to reduce by 300–400 calories every few weeks. Do not aim to drop more than 1½ pounds a week when dieting for a contest.

If you find that you are slimming down too fast, then moderate your diet by eating slightly more to prevent your peak arriving ahead of schedule. Train with heavier weights and shorten your workouts to delay the oncoming peak.

Cut calories by reducing fats drastically. Fat contains 3500 calories per pound while protein and carbohydrates have only about 500. A competition diet should still be balanced. You should eat fresh fruits, vegetables, and whole grains. Potatoes and whole-wheat bread are fine, so long as you leave out the butter and sour cream. Eat more fish and poultry (without the skin) rather than red meats, which contain lots of fat. Dairy products should be greatly curtailed during your countdown; eat none at all during the last few weeks.

Aim to peak a week before the show and then fine tune your condition by balancing your diet. Have a photo session during the last week prior to competing.

Carbing Up

Ten years ago, bodybuilders prepared for competitions by completely cutting out carbohydrates from their diets during the last two or three weeks prior to a contest. The problem with this was that it left them with little energy for training. It also made their muscles look flat and stringy due to a lack of glycogen in them. Bodybuilders of today follow a low-carbohydrate diet for the last week, but then "carb up" by eating small, frequent amounts of complex carbohydrates (such as baked potato, rice, or pasta) during the final three or four days before competing. This "carbing up" will replace depleted glycogen into the muscles so they will appear full.

Water is both the bodybuilder's friend and foe. At the time you are being judged in a contest, you need water in your muscles to plump out the cells. You do not want water under the skin. For the last week before a competition, avoid eating salt and all foods with salt in them. During the last week you should drink only distilled bottled water and be extremely careful about what foods you eat. Most women find that taking potassium supplements before a competition helps to displace the water under the skin and put it into the muscles where it will help increase mass without loss of definition.

Body Awareness

Since you will be judged from every angle on contest day, it is wise to spend plenty of time during the last two months before a show being self-critical of how your body looks. Set up two full-length mirrors so that you can study yourself from all angles. Increase your body awareness not just by posing but also by studying yourself in the "relaxed" positions. (The relaxed round is a mis-nomer. In actual fact, you tense your muscles just as hard in this round, while in the relaxed posture, as you do in the compulsory poses.)

Training Countdown

Use substantial weights when training prior to a contest, but make a point of concentrating more on form. Rest between sets less than you would during off-season training. Increase workout frequency to five or six days a week. Practice isotension (the flexing of your muscles during and at the conclusion of each rep). Begin or increase aerobic activity, such as stationary bike riding, to help reduce subcutaneous fat. Add exercises to your routine that stress isolation of individual muscles (flyes rather than bench presses; thigh extensions and hack squats rather than regular squats; concentration curls rather than barbell curls). Use dumbbells rather than barbells during the precontest period.

Tanning Up

The lighting on most contest stages is as bright as the sun, so you had better be well tanned if you want to look good to the judges. The darker you are, the harder you will look. Increase your suntanning time as the contest approaches. Not only will it improve your color, but you will slightly improve definition by removing water from just under the skin. Bodybuilder Frank Zane would spend his last few precontest days in the sun for up to eight hours a day. Do not forget to tan all over, including your armpits and on both sides of your arms.

Today most top bodybuilders get their tans by following a three-fold method: (1) sunbathing outside when it's convenient, (2) using sunlamps, and (3) using chemical "quick-tan" preparations. (Dy-O-Derm is the most popular. Owen

Labs Division, Box 1959, Fort Worth, Texas 76101.) If you use a chemical preparation, use rubber gloves and cotton balls to apply these solutions. Cover the entire body, including the face. Several applications may be required over the last two or three days. Do not leave your artificial tanning until the morning of the contest. If you have the skin for it (and the climate), a natural tan is far superior to a chemically simulated tan. Ask Frank Zane, Tom Platz, or Rachel McLish.

Preparing for the Stage

There is much to learn before you step onstage for a contest. Not only must you prepare yourself mentally and physically, it is vital to know what the judges will expect in the preliminary stages of any contest. You had better know what you are doing. Make doubly sure that you know all the compulsory poses by heart, and that you can perform them according to the required rules. The more you practice any pose, the better your muscles will look in that position. In fact, many quite ordinary poses have become personal masterpieces for some women, simply from frequent practice.

Study how to make your body look its best in relaxed positions. You will notice by moving your back, arms, shoulders, etc., that you can bring out more detail in some positions over others. Use your best positions when being judged.

If you are called out by the judges for comparisons with other contestants, walk briskly to the posing area and concentrate on the head judge's directions. Be the *first* to pose when asked. Assume the pose, pan the judges slowly, and stop when requested. This can be a physically draining ordeal, especially if you are called out often. Your prior pos-

ing practice will help; those who have not practiced a lot will find their stamina dwindling. The degree of tenacity or competitive spirit a woman has, as long as it's kept within the boundary of good manners, will help improve her chances of winning.

Free Posing

Your free-posing routine should become second nature by the time the contest takes place. This is your chance to shine. You are free to do whatever poses you wish to the accompaniment of your choice of music. Develop your posing routine by looking at pictures in books and magazines. Study videotapes of the best posers, including Erika Mes, Mary Roberts, Carla Temple, Tina Plakinger, Corinna Everson, Rachel McLish, Penny Price, Carla Dunlap, and many more.

Learn at least 30 different poses, and practice them regularly. Include only your best ones in your routine. Show your best angles from front, back, and sides. Remember that transitions (going from one pose to another) are as important as the poses themselves. You may want to hire a choreographer to help plan your routine, but make sure they understand the requirements of a good bodybuilding posing routine. Remember, the judges are still looking for proportion and muscle definition.

Your music selection should be upbeat and complement your posing style in a dramatic presentation. Record the musical interludes on tape and make a copy just in case it gets lost. You don't want to pose to silence . . . nor to someone else's music.

The most demanding posing session is the posedown. The six finalists will be required to pose together to see who is the best. It's like a free-for-all.

On stage for a competition . . . Rachel McLish is in the middle.

Women step in front of each other, and flex for all they are worth. This is quick and aggressive posing designed to attract the judges' eyes. It is far better to repeat your best six or eight poses than to go through your entire routine. The emphasis is on muscularity. Do not do back poses. You lose eye contact with the judges who will look towards the person doing a front pose.

Contest Pack Bag

1. *Two towels*. Use one for wiping oil from your hands, and the other for use after showering. (Not all backstage areas have shower facilities, however.)
2. *Two costumes*. Wear one for the preliminary judging and one for the free-posing evening show. Be careful not to get oil on them.
3. *Posing oil*. Apricot or almond oil (available at health-food stores) helps tighten the skin. Baby oil reflects back light like a mirror. Apricot and almond oils highlight the muscles.
4. *Tanning Makeup*. Last minute retouches may be necessary, especially if your tan is artificial. Excessive sweating can make it run or even rub off.
5. *Makeup and grooming supplies*. Take a comb, brush, hair spray, makeup, and a small mirror. You may not have access to a mirror backstage.
6. *Rubber shower shoes*. Backstage conditions are often extremely dirty.
7. *Rubber expanders*. Most women pump up before going on stage. Rubber expanders come in useful for pumping shoulders and biceps. Today most show promoters supply some weights for pumping up. But there may not be enough for everyone's use.

We hope that all the information in *Superpump!*—plus the advice from many of the biggest names in women's bodybuilding today—will help to develop and shape your body according to your goals. As you progress and enjoy the health benefits and improvements in your appearance, it is our sincerest wish that you also enjoy the bodybuilding way of life.

About the Authors

Superpump! is the second collaboration between Ben Weider and Robert Kennedy. The first, *Pumping Up!*, was an enormous success in the world of women's bodybuilding.

Ben Weider is a specialist in the field of bodybuilding and physical education. He is a member of the Order of Canada, the highest award made to Canadian citizens. Additionally, he is a member of the national faculty of the United States Sports Academy, secretary general of the International Council of Physical Fitness Research, and a member of the National Advisory Council on Fitness and Amateur Sports. He was elected to the research council of International Council of Sports and Physical Education (UNESCO). Recently, Ben Weider was nominated for the Nobel Peace Prize. He is the elected president of the International Federation of Bodybuilders (IFBB).

During the past quarter of a century, Ben Weider has travelled to over 100 countries. He has met with sports and fitness specialists to help promote fitness and bodybuilding.

"Back in 1934," said Ben, "my brother Joe had a burning desire to develop his body. In spite of having no money, he somehow managed to train with make-do weights. It wasn't long before he had built quite a magnificent physique. When I saw what his workouts had done, I started training, too."

Subsequently, at the age of seventeen, and with only seven dollars to his name, Joe got another inspiration. He wanted to start his own magazine. Issue number one was a simple mimeographed effort, which sold for 10 cents a copy. That same magazine built up in circulation from a handful of copies to the present readership of several million. Today it is known as *Muscle & Fitness* and thanks to Joe's initial inspiration and ongoing creativity, it is now the top-selling specialist magazine in the world. Other successful magazines have been added to the Weider stable, including *Shape*, *Flex*, and *Sports Fitness*.

Ben and Joe were naturals when it came to business. "Those early years were tough," said Ben, "but we had a first-rate creation and it just got better and better." Gradually, product lines were added to the Weider ventures. It was later decided that Joe Weider would open up offices in the United States—first in New York, then in Los Angeles.

Ben opted to stay in Canada, where he concentrated on developing his own sporting goods business in Montreal. His main goal is to spread the sport of bodybuilding and to expand the IFBB even further (it already has chapters in 126 countries, is the sixth-largest sports organization in the world, and is affiliated with the General Assembly of Sports Federations). Additionally, he would like to see bodybuilding as an Olympic event. He has been working towards this end for some time and, if perseverance has anything to do with it, success is not far away.

The IFBB organization crosses many ideological boundaries. Its credo is sim-

Robert Kennedy and Ben Weider

ple yet meaningful: "Bodybuilding is good for nation building." Ben Weider was in communist China long before the arrival of the celebrated table tennis players, and as the invited guest of that country's ministry of sports. His record speaks for itself.

Ben trains regularly with weights, three times a week. He also does 300 push-ups and 200 sit-ups every day. He is happily married to a beautiful French-Canadian, Hugette, and is the father of three children.

As well as his previous book on women's bodybuilding, *Pumping Up!*, co-authored with Robert Kennedy, he has also authored several others, all best sellers. Titles include *Fit for Life*, *The Strongest Man in History*, *Louis Cyr*, and the *Murder of Napoleon*. The latter is currently being made into a film.

Robert Kennedy was brought up in England by parents who were teachers. His mother is English and his father is Austrian. He attended his parents' private school in Thetford, Norfolk, then passed his exams to Culford Public School near Bury St. Edmonds, Suffolk. After obtaining his school certificates, he then went on to Norwich College of Art, where he obtained the highest British government art award: the National Diploma in Design, specializing in oil painting and sculpture. In addition, he attended Sheffield Art College, gaining his art teacher's diploma, then universities in Salzburg, Austria; Lausanne, Switzerland; and the Loughborough Physical Training College in England. After seven years teaching at the college level in London, Robert emigrated to Canada in 1967 and founded his own bodybuilding magazine *Musclemag International*. From the beginning, circulation grew rapidly. "*Musclemag International* is a considerably smaller voice than Weider's *Muscle & Fitness*," said Kennedy, "but we do our best to supply the training needs of serious male and female bodybuilders. We have a strong core of loyal subscribers from all over the world."

As one might expect from his art background and passion for sculpture, Robert has a personal interest in the graphics of his magazine as well as the features and photographs that are run within its pages. He still paints and is planning a series of one-man exhibitions in Toronto, New York, and London. Already he has exhibited in Canada, Britain, France, and Austria.

His zealous interest in bodybuilding started in art college at the age of eighteen. He has been training regularly ever since. "It's been thirty years!" he said. "The only contests I ever won were the college weightlifting championships and the Cannes Film Festival bodybuilding championships held in the south of France." He did train extremely hard for twenty years, but he is not a genetic superior when it comes to bodybuilding.

His avid interest and practical knowledge over all the years has made Robert Kennedy an authority on bodybuilding. He has written fifteen books on the subject to date, including *Start Bodybuilding*, *Hardcore Bodybuilding*, *Beef It!*, and *Reps!* (all published by Sterling Publishing Co., Two Park Avenue, New York, NY 10016).

Like co-author Ben Weider, Robert Kennedy is a friend to many of the world's top competing bodybuilders and he is an acknowledged supporter of the IFBB and Ben's tireless effort to promote bodybuilding around the world.

Index